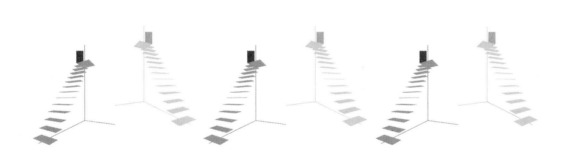

KÖNEMANN

© 2019 koenemann.com GmbH
www.koenemann.com

ÉDITIONS
PLACE DES
VICTOIRES

© Éditions Place des Victoires
6, rue du Mail – 75002 Paris
www.victoires.com

ISBN : 978-2-8099-1684-3
Dépôt légal : 2ᵉ trimestre 2019

Editorial project: © LOFT Publications S.L.
loft@loftpublications.com

Editorial coordinator: Claudia Martínez Alonso
Art director: Mireia Casanovas Soley
Assistant to editorial coordination: Ana Marques
Edition and texts: Marta Serrats
Translations: textcase

ISBN: 978-3-7419-2381-4 (international)

Printed in China by Shenzhen Hua Xin Colour-printing & Platemaking Co., Ltd

This book offers a broad and practical view of minimalist home design, with numerous examples.

In architecture and interior design, the term "minimalist" means simplicity and moderation, with spacious flat surfaces that evoke serenity and industrial or simple materials. Another central tenet is the importance of light and its effect on interior spaces. Minimalist decor allows more emphasis on textures. Forms are as pure as possible and defined by geometric designs. Functionality and its relationship with the surroundings are paramount.

The most common interior colour scheme is a combination of white with vivid colours, such as red or black, to create a stark contrast. Natural and prefabricated materials are used for simple furnishings. Designers choose furniture with pure lines, made with unprocessed materials. Concrete, glass, and metal play an important role in the design of these spaces.

The concept of minimalism has evolved in recent years, resulting in what is known as *new minimalism*, which breaks away from an austere aesthetic. Designers now introduce small colour variations to satisfy the tastes of those who found the austere look unwelcoming. This evolution is reflected in the following pages, where fans of this trend can discover the infinite possibilities of minimalism.

L'objectif de ce livre est d'offrir une vision large et pratique du minimalisme à travers une foule d'exemples d'habitats inspirés par ce concept.

Dans le domaine de l'architecture et de la décoration intérieure, la notion de minimalisme s'applique à ces créations aux aménagements simples et mesurés, aux surfaces vastes et planes évoquant la sérénité, réalisées avec des matériaux industriels ou de manufacture simple. D'autres enjeux importants sont la mise en valeur de la lumière et son effet sur les volumes et les espaces intérieurs des édifices. La décoration est réduite au minimum pour céder le pas à la revalorisation des textures. Les formes, aussi pures que possible, se caractérisent par un design géométrique. La fonctionnalité revêt une importance particulière, tout comme la relation avec l'environnement.

En décoration intérieure, le schéma classique consiste à combiner du blanc avec des couleurs intenses, comme le rouge ou le noir, pour créer un contraste marqué. On utilise autant des matériaux naturels que manufacturés pour instaurer une décoration simple. En ce qui concerne le mobilier, on recherche des meubles aux lignes épurées et donc des matériaux non traités. Le béton, le verre et le métal font partie intégrante du design de ces espaces.

Le concept a évolué ces dernières années avec ce que l'on appelle le *nouveau minimalisme*, qui se détache de l'esthétique dépouillée et introduit de petites variations chromatiques pour satisfaire aux goûts des personnes qui trouvent ce style trop froid, une évolution reflétée dans les pages suivantes, pour faire découvrir aux adeptes de ce courant les possibilités infinies qu'offre le minimalisme.

Ziel dieses Buches ist es, eine umfassende und praktische Sichtweise des Minimalismus anhand zahlreicher Beispiele von Wohnungen, die sich auf dieses Konzept stützen, zu schaffen.

Im Bereich der Architektur und Innenarchitektur wird die minimalistische Bezeichnung auf die Werke übertragen, die Schlichtheit und maßvolle Entwürfe aufzeigen, mit weiten ebenen Flächen, die Gelassenheit ausstrahlen und die mit Industriematerialien sowie in einfacher Herstellung geschaffen wurden. Eine andere wichtige Grundvoraussetzung ist die Analyse des Lichts und seine Wirkung auf das Volumen und die Räume im Inneren der Gebäude. Die Dekoration reduziert sich auf das Minimale, um die Strukturen neu zu bewerten. Die Formen zeigen sich in ihrer reinsten Erscheinung und definieren sich in geometrischen Designs. Es wird großen Wert auf die Funktionalität und vor allem auf die Verbindung zu ihrer Umgebung gelegt.

In der Innenarchitektur ist das meist benutzte Schema die Kombination aus weißen und intensiven Farben, wie Rot und Schwarz, um einen extremen Kontrast herzustellen. Es werden sowohl natürliche wie auch vorgefertigte Materialien benutzt, die eine schlichte Verzierung ermöglichen. Hinsichtlich des Mobiliars wird auf eine reine Linienführung mithilfe von beruhigenden Materialien gezielt. Beton, Glas und Metall sind Teil des Design dieser Räume.

Das Konzept hat sich in den letzten Jahren in den sogenannten *Neuen Minimalismus* verwandelt, der mit der nüchternen Ästhetik bricht und für kleine Veränderungen in der Farbgebung sorgt, um den Vorlieben jener Personen gerecht zu werden, die ihn für weniger gemütlich hielten. Dieser Wandel spiegelt sich auf den folgenden Seiten wider, in denen die Liebhaber dieser Bewegung auf unzählige Möglichkeiten, die der Minimalismus bietet, stoßen werden.

De opzet van dit boek is een uitgebreide en praktische visie bieden op het minimalisme op basis van talloze voorbeelden van woningen die zijn geïnspireerd op minimalistische principes.

Op het gebied van architectuur en binnenhuisinrichting wordt het concept minimalisme toegepast op creaties die in de opzet van het ontwerp blijk geven van eenvoud en ingetogenheid. Kenmerkend zijn de ruime oppervlaktes die sereniteit uitstralen en die ingericht worden met industriële of handgemaakte materialen. Een ander belangrijk uitgangspunt is de waarde die toegekend wordt aan het licht en het effect daarvan op de ruimtes in het interieur van een gebouw. De aankleding wordt tot een minimum beperkt om plaats te maken voor de herwaardering van de texturen. Vormen worden in geometrische ontwerpen in hun puurste vorm weergegeven. Er wordt veel belang gehecht aan functionaliteit en aan de relatie met de natuurlijke omgeving.

Bij de binnenhuisarchitectuur wordt vooral een kleurenschema toegepast van wit tegenover intense kleuren zoals rood en zwart om een opvallend contrast te creëren. Er worden zowel natuurlijke als voorgefabriceerde materialen gebruikt die zorgen voor een eenvoudige inrichting. Wat het meubilair betreft, wordt zuiverheid van lijnen in niet bewerkte materialen nagestreefd. Beton, glas en metaal vormen steeds de basis voor het interieur.

Het concept is de laatste jaren geëvolueerd naar wat we nu *nieuw minimalisme* noemen. Deze nieuwe uiting breekt met de sobere esthetiek en introduceert kleine kleurvariaties om te beantwoorden aan de smaak van mensen die het zuivere minimalisme niet aantrekkelijk vinden. Deze evolutie komt duidelijk tot uiting op de volgende pagina's waar liefhebbers van deze stroming de ontelbare mogelijkheden van het minimalisme zullen ontdekken.

El objetivo de este libro es ofrecer una visión amplia y práctica del minimalismo a través de numerosos ejemplos de viviendas inspiradas en este concepto.

En el ámbito de la arquitectura y el diseño de interiores, el término *minimalista* se aplica a aquellas creaciones que muestran sencillez y mesura en su planteamiento, con amplias superficies planas que evocan serenidad y que están realizadas con materiales industriales o de manufactura simple. Otras premisas importantes son la valoración de la luz y su efecto en los volúmenes y espacios interiores de los edificios. La decoración se reduce al mínimo para dar paso a la revalorización de las texturas. Las formas se presentan lo más puras posible y se definen en diseños geométricos. Se da especial importancia a la funcionalidad y sobre todo a su relación con el entorno.

En interiorismo, el esquema más utilizado es la combinación del blanco con colores intensos como el rojo o el negro para crear un contraste marcado. Se emplean tanto materiales naturales como prefabricados que permitan una ornamentación sencilla. Por lo que respecta al mobiliario, se busca una pureza de líneas mediante el uso de materiales no alterados. El hormigón, el vidrio y el metal son habituales en el diseño de estos espacios.

En los últimos años, el concepto ha evolucionado hacia el denominado *nuevo minimalismo*, que rompe con la estética austera e introduce pequeñas variaciones de color para satisfacer los gustos de aquellas personas que lo encontraban poco acogedor. Esta evolución se refleja en las siguientes páginas, donde los amantes de esta corriente descubrirán las posibilidades infinitas que brinda el minimalismo.

L'obiettivo di questo libro è offrire una visione ampia e pratica del minimalismo tramite numerosi esempi di case che si ispirano a questo concetto.

Nell'ambito dell'architettura e del design d'interni, il termine *minimalista* si applica a quelle creazioni che mostrano semplicità e misura nel loro progetto, con ampie superfici piane che evocano serenità e che sono realizzate con materiali industriali o di manifattura semplice. Altre premesse importanti sono la valorizzazione della luce e del suo effetto nei volumi e negli spazi interni degli edifici. L'arredamento è ridotto al minimo per dare spazio alla rivalutazione delle trame. Le forme si presentano più pure possibili e si manifestano con disegni geometrici. È data particolare importanza alla funzionalità e soprattutto al suo rapporto con l'ambiente.

Nel design d'interni, il modello più utilizzato è la combinazione del bianco con colori intensi come il rosso o il nero per creare un contrasto marcato. Sono impiegati sia materiali naturali, sia prefabbricati che consentano una decorazione semplice. Per quanto riguarda i mobili, si ricerca la purezza di linee attraverso l'uso di materiali non trattati. Il cemento, il vetro e il metallo fanno parte del design di questi spazi.

Il concetto si è sviluppato negli ultimi anni in ciò che è conosciuto come il *nuovo minimalismo*, che abbandona l'estetica austera e introduce piccole modifiche di colore per soddisfare i gusti di quanti lo consideravano poco accogliente. Questa evoluzione è rispecchiata nelle pagine successive, dove gli amanti di questa corrente scopriranno le infinite possibilità che il minimalismo offre.

O objetivo deste livro é proporcionar uma visão ampla e prática do minimalismo, através de numerosos exemplos de casas inspiradas neste conceito.

Na área da arquitetura e da decoração de interiores, o termo *minimalista* aplica-se a criações com uma conceção regida pela simplicidade e a parcimónia, com amplas superfícies planas que evocam serenidade, conseguidas com materiais industriais ou de manufatura simples. Outros elementos importantes são a valorização da luz e do seu efeito sobre os volumes e espaços interiores dos edifícios. A decoração é reduzida ao mínimo, dando lugar a uma revalorização das texturas. As formas são o mais puras possível e definem-se segundo esquemas geométricos. Atribui-se especial importância à funcionalidade e sobretudo à relação com o meio envolvente.

Em decoração, o esquema mais utilizado consiste na combinação do branco com cores vivas, como o vermelho ou o negro, para criar contrastes bem marcados. Usam-se materiais, tanto naturais como prefabricados, que permitam uma ornamentação simples. No que respeita ao mobiliário, procura-se a pureza das linhas, através do uso de materiais não processados. O betão, o vidro e o metal são utilizados na conceção destes espaços.

O conceito evoluiu nos últimos anos, com o chamado *novo minimalismo*, que rompe com a austeridade estética e introduz pequenas variações de cor, de modo a satisfazer o gosto daqueles que o consideravam pouco acolhedor. Esta evolução reflete-se nas páginas seguintes, onde os apreciadores desta tendência poderão descobrir a infinidade de possibilidades que o minimalismo permite.

Syftet med den här boken är att ge en bred och praktisk presentation av minimalismen genom många exempel på bostäder som inspirerats av detta tankesätt.

Inom arkitektur och inredning avser termen *minimalism* verk som är enkla och återhållsamt planerade, med stora öppna ytor som ger lugn och som genomförs i industriella material eller med enkla tillverkningssätt. Andra viktiga inslag är att man värdesätter ljuset och dess effekt i byggnadernas interiör och inredning. Inredningen begränsas till ett minimum för att ge plats för en återupptäckt av alla texturer. Formerna som används är de renaste möjliga och de uttrycks ofta i geometriska mönster. Man betonar särskilt funktionalitet och framför allt förhållandet till den omgivande miljön.

Inom inredning är det vanligaste en kombinationen av vitt med starka färger som rött eller svart för att skapa en skarp kontrast. Man använder både naturliga och prefabricerade material som bidrar till enkel utsmyckning. I möblerna söker man rena linjer och material som manipulerats så lite som möjligt. Betong, glas och metall är vanligt i utformningen av miljöerna.

Konceptet har under de senaste åren utvecklats till den så kallade *nyminimalismen* som bryter av med stram estetik men introducerar färgvariationer för att passa människor som annars finner stilen ogästvänlig. Den trenden återspeglas på de kommande sidorna, där anhängare av den här stilen kommer att upptäcka minimalismens oändliga möjligheter.

ORFILA FLAT

SCHNEIDER COLAO ARCHITECTS // Madrid, Spain
© Diego Domínguez

This 200-square-metre (2150 square-feet) apartment, in a 19th-century building in Madrid's Chamberí district, was completely reconstructed to create an open space merging the different rooms. The owners, who practice yoga and meditation, wanted movement through the house to be fluid and intuitive.

Cet appartement de 200 m², situé dans un édifice du XIXᵉ siècle du quartier madrilène de Chamberí, a été totalement rénové pour créer un espace ouvert fusionnant des pièces bien distinctes. Les propriétaires, qui pratiquent le yoga et la méditation, désiraient que
le passage dans la maison soit fluide et intuitif.

Diese Wohnung auf 200 m² wurde in ein Gebäude aus dem 19. Jahrhundert in Chamberí, einem Stadtteil von Madrid, gebaut und komplett wiederhergestellt, um einen offenen Raum, der die verschiedenen Bereiche miteinander verknüpft, zu schaffen. Die Besitzer, die Yoga und Meditation praktizieren, wollten, dass die Zirkulation des Hauses fließend und intuitiv ist

Dit appartement van 200 m² bevindt zich in een gebouw uit de negentiende eeuw in de Madrileense wijk Chamberí. Het werd volledig gerenoveerd om een open ruimte te creëren en zo de verschillende vertrekken in elkaar over te laten gaan. De eigenaren die aan yoga en meditatie doen, wilden zich naar hun gevoel vloeiend door de ruimte kunnen bewegen.

Este piso de 200 m², situado en un edificio del siglo XIX del barrio madrileño de Chamberí, fue completamente reconstruido para crear un espacio abierto que fusionara las distintas estancias. Los propietarios, que practican el yoga y la meditación, querían que la circulación por la casa fuera fluida e intuitiva.

Questo appartamento di 200 m², situato in un edificio del XIX secolo nel quartiere madrileno di Chamberí, è stato ricostruito completamente per creare uno spazio aperto che comprendesse le varie stanze. I proprietari, che praticano yoga e meditazione, volevano che la circolazione nella casa fosse fluida e intuitiva.

Este andar de 200 m², situado num edifício do século XIX do bairro madrileno de Chamberí, foi completamente reconstruído, de modo a criar um espaço aberto em que se fundem as diversas divisões. Os proprietários, praticantes de ioga e meditação, queriam que a circulação através da casa fosse fluida e intuitiva.

Denna våning på 200 m², i en 1800-talsbyggnad i Madrids stadsdel Chamberí, byggdes om helt för att skapa ett öppet utrymme som förenar de olika rummen. Ägarna, som praktiserar yoga och meditation, ville att rörelsen genom huset skulle vara smidig och intuitiv.

Glass has steadily been taking over from brick: solid, opaque walls have given way to transparent walls and large windows, which offer a permanent connection to the outdoors.

Le verre a supplanté la brique : les murs ont été remplacés par des parois transparentes et de grandes baies vitrées offrant un lien permanent avec l'extérieur.

Glas ist dem Ziegelstein zuvorgekommen und die Mauern haben sich in transparente Wände und große Fenster verwandelt, die eine ständige Verbindung zur Außenwelt bieten.

Glas wint steeds meer terrein op baksteen. Muren worden transparante wanden en grote ramen die een permanente verbinding met de buitenwereld vormen.

El cristal ha ido ganando terreno al ladrillo y los muros se han convertido en paredes transparentes y grandes ventanales que ofrecen una conexión permanente con el exterior.

Il vetro ha guadagnato terreno sul mattone e i muri sono stati trasformati in pareti trasparenti e grandi finestroni, che offrono un collegamento permanente con l'esterno.

O vidro foi ganhando terreno ao tijolo e as paredes foram substituídas por divisórias transparentes e grandes janelões, que permitem uma permanente ligação com o exterior.

Glas har börjat knappa in på tegel och murar har förvandlats till transparenta väggar och stora fönster, som erbjuder en permanent anslutning till världen utanför.

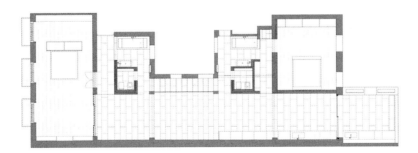

Floor plan

The simplicity of materials is a fundamental requirement for achieving a minimalist look. Choose natural materials such as Macael marble or Dinesen wood.

La simplicité des matériaux est l'un des principes de base du minimalisme. Choisissez des éléments naturels comme le marbre de Macael ou le bois Dinesen.

Die Einfachheit der Materialien ist eines der Merkmale des Minimalismus. Wählen Sie natürliche Elemente wie Macael-Marmor oder Dinesen-Holz.

De eenvoud van materialen is een van de uitgangspunten van het minimalisme. Kies voor natuurlijke elementen zoals marmer van Macael of Dinesen hout.

La simplicidad de los materiales es una de las premisas del minimalismo. Opta por elementos naturales como el mármol de Macael o la madera Dinesen.

La semplicità dei materiali è una delle premesse del minimalismo. Preferisci elementi naturali come il marmo di Macael o il legno Dinesen.

A simplicidade de materiais é um dos princípios do minimalismo. Opte por elementos naturais, como o mármore de Macael e a madeira Dienesen.

Enkla material är en av minimalismens förutsättningar. Välj naturliga inslag som marmor från Macael eller Dinesens trä.

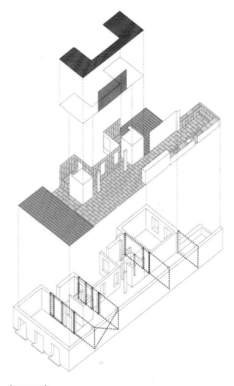

Axonometric

HOUSEWING

MINSOO LEE, KEEHYUN AHN / ANL STUDIO // Seoul, South Korea
© Sunghwan Yoon, Heebon Koo

Living and working areas can occupy the same space, as in this Seoul artist's renovated apartment. A striking white wing crosses the house, differentiating these two facets of life and maximising the sense of space.

Deux activités distinctes, en l'occurrence vivre et travailler, peuvent cohabiter dans le même espace comme le démontre cet appartement de Séoul, rénové par un artiste. Du design se détache cette sorte d'aile blanche qui traverse le lieu, créée pour différencier ces deux facettes de la vie combinées ici et maximiser
la perception de l'espace.

Zwei so verschiedene Aktivitäten wie Leben und Arbeit können auf einem Raum nebeneinander existieren, wie es diese Wohnung in Seoul zeigt, die für einen Künstler renoviert wurde. Aus dem Design sticht der weiße Flügel, der das Haus kreuzt, hervor, der die zwei Facetten des Lebens differenzieren und die räumliche Wahrnehmung vergrößern sollte.

Dit appartement in Seoul, gerenoveerd door een kunstenaar, laat zien dat twee verschillende activiteiten als werken en wonen goed samengaan. Opvallend aan het ontwerp is de witte vleugel die de woning doorkruist. Deze stelt de twee tegengestelde levensfacetten voor en creëert een maximale ruimtelijke perceptie.

Dos actividades tan distintas como vivir y trabajar pueden cohabitar un mismo espacio, como muestra este apartamento de Seúl, renovado para un artista. Del diseño destaca el ala blanca que cruza la casa, pensada para diferenciar estas dos facetas enfrentadas de la vida y para maximizar la percepción espacial.

Due attività così diverse come vivere e lavorare possono coesistere in uno stesso spazio, come dimostra questo appartamento di Seul, ristrutturato da un artista. Del progetto spicca l'ala bianca che attraversa la casa, pensata per distinguere questi due aspetti contrastanti della vita e per aumentare al massimo la percezione spaziale.

Duas atividades tão diferentes como viver e trabalhar podem conviver no mesmo espaço, como prova este apartamento remodelado para um artista, em Seul. Destaca-se neste projeto a asa branca que atravessa a casa, concebida para separar estas duas facetas da vida e maximizar a perceção do espaço.

Två så skilda aktiviteter som boende och arbete kan samsas om samma utrymme, vilket den här lägenheten i Söul, som renoverats för en konstnär, visar. Det som framträder i designen är den vita vingen tvärs igenom huset, som är utformad att skilja de två aspekterna av livet åt och att maximera rumsuppfattningen.

Striking angular lines offer a highly contemporary minimalist look. The structure's ergonomic arrangement facilitates movement.

Les lignes saillantes et anguleuses offrent une esthétique minimaliste très contemporaine. Le jeu ergonomique de la structure apporte du mouvement.

Hervorstehende und verwinkelte Linien schaffen eine minimalistische und sehr zeitgenössische Ästhetik. Das ergonomische Spiel der Struktur bringt Bewegung.

De uitspringende en hoekige lijnen zorgen voor een zeer eigentijds, minimalistisch interieur. Dit ergonomisch spel brengt beweging in de structuur.

Las líneas salientes y anguladas ofrecen una estética minimalista muy contemporánea. El juego ergonómico de la estructura aporta movimiento.

Le linee sporgenti e angolate offrono un'estetica minimalista molto contemporanea. Il gioco ergonomico della struttura apporta movimento.

As linhas salientes e angulosas proporcionam uma estética minimalista muito contemporânea. O jogo ergonómico da estrutura transmite movimento.

Utstående och vinklade linjer ger ett mycket modernt och minimalistiskt utseende. Strukturens ergonomi ger också en rörelse.

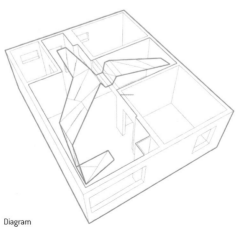

Diagram

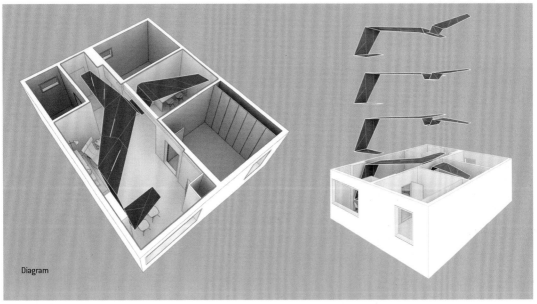

Diagram

Use modular furniture that can be integrated into the structure. This will produce a room that feels open.

Choisissez un mobilier modulaire qui s'intègre à la structure. Vous obtiendrez un espace plus dégagé.

Greifen Sie auf ein modulares Mobiliar zurück, das sich in die Struktur integriert. Sie werden ein weiträumiges Zimmer erschaffen.

Opteer voor modulaire meubels die zich integreren in de structuur. Zo creëer je ruimte en overzicht.

Recurre a un mobiliario modular que se integre en la estructura. Conseguirás una habitación despejada.

Impiega mobili modulari che si integrino nella struttura. Otterrai una stanza spaziosa.

Opte por um mobiliário modular que se integre na estrutura. Vai deste modo conseguir uma casa desafogada.

Man använder modulmöbler som integreras i strukturen. Det gör bostaden rymlig.

GLAZED APARTMENT

SERGI PONS // Barcelona, Spain
© Adrià Goula

The remodelling of this apartment in the Gràcia district of Barcelona was structured around a perforated brick wall. This barrier divides the apartment into clearly differentiated zones (daytime and nighttime), creating visual relationships between them. As requested by the client, citrus yellow provides a cold, almost acidic touch to the atmosphere.

La rénovation de cet appartement du quartier barcelonais de Gràcia se structure autour d'un mur en briques perforées. Cette barrière divise l'appartement en deux zones clairement définies (de jour et de nuit) tout en créant une continuité visuelle entre elles. Le jaune citron apporte à l'ambiance une touche froide, presque acide, recherchée par le client.

Die Renovierung dieser Wohnung in Gràcia, einem Stadtteil von Barcelona, wird um eine Lochsteinmauer gegliedert. Diese Mauer teilt die Wohnung in zwei klar differenzierte Teile (Tag und Nacht) und schafft zwischen ihnen eine visuelle Verbindung. Das Zitronengelb schafft eine kühle, fast bissige Atmosphäre, die der Kunde wünschte.

Bij de verbouwing van deze flat in de wijk Gràcia in Barcelona is een muur van holle baksteen centraal komen te staan die de woning in twee duidelijk verschillende zones (dag en nacht) verdeelt, maar ze wel visueel verbindt. Het citroengeel zorgt voor de koele, lichtelijk zure toets die de cliënt voor ogen had.

La reforma de este piso del barrio barcelonés de Gràcia se estructura en torno a un muro de ladrillo gero. Esta barrera divide el apartamento en dos zonas claramente diferenciadas (día y noche), creando relaciones visuales entre ellas. El amarillo cítrico aporta a la atmósfera el toque frío, casi ácido, que el cliente deseaba.

La ristrutturazione di questo appartamento del quartiere barcellonese di Gràcia è impostata attorno a un muro di mattoni forati. Questa barriera divide l'appartamento in due zone nettamente differenziate (giorno e notte), creando collegamenti visivi fra le stesse. Il giallo limone conferisce all'atmosfera il tocco freddo, quasi acido, che desiderava il cliente.

A remodelação deste andar no bairro de Gràcia, em Barcelona, foi estruturada em torno de uma parede em tijolo furado. Esta barreira divide o apartamento em duas zonas claramente diferenciadas (dia e noite), criando relações visuais entre elas. O amarelo-citrino confere ao ambiente o toque frio, quase ácido, que o cliente pretendia.

Renoveringen av den här lägenheten i stadsdelen Gràcia i Barcelona är uppbyggd kring väggen av håltegel. Barriären delar in lägenheten i två klart avskilda skilda områden (dag och natt), och skapar visuella relationer mellan dem. Det citrongula ger atmosfären en kall, nästan sur, touche som kunden ville ha.

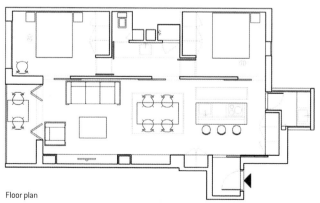

Floor plan

Bear in mind that the harmony of a space can be destroyed if even one object does not go with the others. Choose similar materials and colours.

N'oubliez pas qu'un seul objet mal assorti peut détruire l'harmonie de l'ensemble. Choisissez des matériaux et des couleurs similaires.

Beachten Sie, dass nur ein einziges Objekt, das nicht zu den anderen passt, die Harmonie des Gesamtkomplexes zerstört. Wählen Sie ähnliche Materialien und Farben.

Een enkel object dat uit de toon valt bij de rest kan de harmonie verstoren. Stem daarom kleuren en materialen op elkaar af.

Ten en cuenta que tan solo un objeto que no vaya con los demás puede destruir la armonía del conjunto. Opta por materiales y colores similares.

Pensa che basta un solo oggetto che non s'intona con il resto per distruggere l'armonia dell'insieme. Scegli materiali e colori simili.

Lembre-se de que basta um único objeto que destoe dos outros para destruir a harmonia de todo o conjunto. Opte por materiais e cores semelhantes.

Tänk på att ett enda föremål som inte passar in kan förstöra harmonin i helheten. Välj liknande material och färger.

AN URBAN REFUGE

SERGI PONS // Barcelona, Spain
© Adrià Goula

At the heart of this apartment in the Eixample district of Barcelona is a room dedicated to ironing—an activity that the owner spends a lot of time on. The colours range from the pine flooring to the yellow of the mobile objects. Decor is not necessary, because the furniture itself functions as decorative features.

Le cœur de cet appartement, situé dans l'Eixample de Barcelone, est la salle de repassage, une activité qu'affectionne le propriétaire. La gamme chromatique de l'appartement se limite au sol en pin à quelques touches de jaune. La décoration est superflue dans la mesure où les meubles en eux-mêmes servent d'éléments décoratifs.

Zentrum dieser Wohnung, die im Eixample in Barcelona liegt, ist der Bügelraum, eine Tätigkeit, mit der der Besitzer sehr viel Zeit verbrachte. Die Farbpalette der Wohnung variiert zwischen den Kiefernfarben des Bodens und dem Gelb der beweglichen Objekte. Die Dekoration ist hier nicht nötig, da dieselben Möbel als Dekorationselemente dienen.

Het hart van deze flat, gelegen in de Eixample wijk van Barcelona, is de strijkkamer. De eigenaar besteedt namelijk veel tijd aan strijken. Het kleurengamma in de woning wisselt van het vurenhout op de vloer tot het geel van de beweegbare objecten. Omdat de meubels dienst doen als decoratieve elementen is decoratie verder overbodig.

El corazón de este piso situado en l'Eixample de Barcelona es la sala de plancha, actividad a la que el propietario dedica mucho tiempo. La gama cromática del apartamento se mueve entre el pino del suelo y el amarillo de los objetos móviles. La decoración no es necesaria, pues los mismos muebles funcionan como elementos decorativos.

Il cuore di questo appartamento situato nell'Eixample di Barcellona è la stireria, attività cui il proprietario dedica molto tempo. La gamma cromatica dell'appartamento passa dal pino del pavimento, al giallo degli oggetti mobili. La decorazione non è necessaria, perché gli stessi mobili fungono da elementi decorativi.

O coração deste andar situado no Eixample de Barcelona é a sala de passar a ferro, atividade a que o proprietário dedica muito tempo. A escala cromática do apartamento varia da cor de pinho do chão ao amarelo dos objetos móveis. Não é necessária qualquer decoração, uma vez que os próprios móveis funcionam como elementos decorativos.

Hjärtat i denna lägenhet belägen i stadsdelen Eixample i Barcelona är strykrummet, en aktivitet som ägaren ägnar mycket tid åt. Den monokroma färgskalan i lägenheten rör sig mellan furu i golvet och gult på flyttbara föremål. Ingen dekoration krävs för möblerna fungerar som dekorativa element.

Mixing visible textures such as steel, wood, and polyurethane will highlight the distinguishing feature of each material.

Mélangez les textures bien visibles comme, par exemple, l'acier, le bois ou le polyuréthane. Vous mettrez en valeur ce qui caractérise et distingue chaque matériau.

Mischen Sie sichtbare Texturen wie zum Beispiel Stahl, Holz oder Polyurethan. Sie werden jedes kleinste Unterscheidungsmerkmal der verschiedenen Materialien hervorheben.

Combineer materialen van zichtbaar verschillende textuur, zoals staal, hout of polyurethaan. Daardoor versterk je de eigenheid van elk materiaal.

Mezcla texturas visibles como el acero, la madera o el poliuretano. Intensificarás la particularidad distintiva de cada material.

Combina trame visibili come l'acciaio, il legno o il poliuretano. Enfatizzerai la particolarità che distingue ogni materiale.

Misture texturas percetíveis, como o aço, a madeira e o poliuretano. Desse modo, intensifica os traços distintivos de cada material.

Blanda synliga texturer, till exempel järn, trä och polyuretan. Det kommer att intensifiera de utmärkande egenskaperna hos varje material.

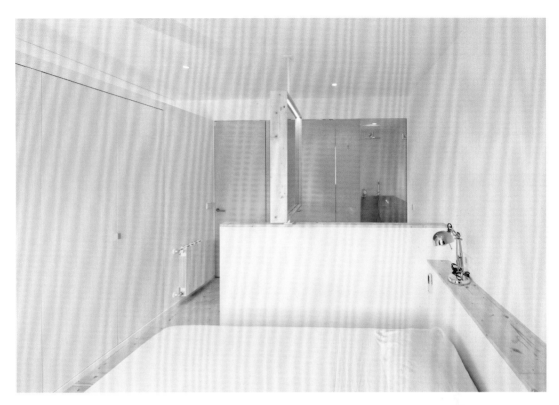

A rotating mirror separates the bed from the bathroom behind the yellow doors.

Un miroir pivotant sépare la chambre de la salle de bains qui se situe derrière ces portes jaunes.

Ein Drehspiegel trennt das Bett vom Badezimmer, das hinter den gelben Türen liegt.

Een draaiende spiegel scheidt het bed van de badruimte die zich achter de gele deuren bevindt.

Un espejo giratorio separa la cama de la zona del baño, situado tras las puertas amarillas.

Uno specchio rotante separa il letto dalla zona del bagno, collocato dietro le porte gialle.

A cama fica separada da zona da casa de banho por um espelho giratório situado por trás das portas amarelas.

En vändbar spegel skiljer sängen från badrumsdelen, som ligger bakom de gula dörrarna.

CASA G+S

GROOPPO // Albissola Marina, Italy

© Anna Positano

Memories of the original building guided the restoration of one of the three apartments in this 19th-century Italian house. One feature stands out: the hexagonal tiles that cover the floor. These imitate the original flooring and emphasise spatial continuity with their variety of colours and shapes.

C'est le souvenir du bâtiment d'origine qui a guidé la rénovation de l'un des trois appartements de cette maison italienne du XIXe siècle. Un élément se démarque tout particulièrement de l'ensemble : les carreaux hexagonaux du sol, imitant le carrelage d'origine, qui soulignent la continuité des espaces avec ses couleurs et ses formes variées.

Es war die Erinnerung an das Originalgebäude, das die Restaurierung einer der drei Wohnungen dieses italienischen Hauses aus dem 19. Jahrhundert veranlasste. Ein Element sticht aus den anderen heraus: die hexagonalen Fliesen, die den Boden bedecken, eine Imitation des Originalfußbodens, der mit seiner Vielfalt an Farben und Formen die Kontinuität des Raumes hervorhebt.

Bij de restauratie van een van de drie verdiepingen van dit Italiaanse huis uit de negentiende eeuw bleef de herinnering aan het oorspronkelijke gebouw intact. Wat opvalt is de vloer van zeshoekige tegels, kopieën van de originele vloertegels, die door hun veelkleurigheid en vorm de voortgang van de ruimtes benadrukken.

Fue el recuerdo del edificio original el que guió la restauración de uno de los tres pisos de esta casa italiana del siglo XIX. Un elemento destaca sobre los demás: los azulejos hexagonales que recubren el suelo, imitación del pavimento original, que con su variedad de colores y formas enfatizan la continuidad de los espacios.

Il ricordo dell'edificio originale è stato ciò che ha guidato la ristrutturazione di uno dei tre piani di questa casa italiana del XIX secolo. Un elemento spicca sul resto: le piastrelle esagonali che rivestono il pavimento, a imitazione di quello originale, che grazie alla varietà di colori e forme accentuano la continuità degli spazi.

Foi a memória do edifício original que inspirou o restauro de um dos três andares desta casa italiana do século XIX. Há um elemento que se destaca de todos os outros: os azulejos hexagonais que revestem o chão, imitação do pavimento original, que, com a suavidade das suas cores e formas, enfatizam a continuidade dos espaços.

Det var minnet av den ursprungliga byggnaden som blev vägledande i restaureringen av en av de tre våningarna i detta italienska 1800-talshus. En sak sticker ut mer än de andra: de sexkantiga plattorna som täcker golvet, en imitation av det ursprungliga golvet, som med variation av färger och former betonar kontinuiteten mellan rummen.

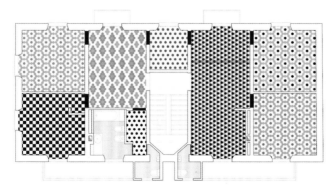

Floor plan

Uniformity and symmetry
are achieved through the
juxtaposition of variously colored
porcelain tiles in seven of the
eight rooms.

L'uniformité et la symétrie
sont obtenues grâce au jeu
chromatique des carreaux de
porcelaine que l'on retrouve
dans sept des huit pièces.

Die Gleichförmigkeit und
Symmetrie wird durch ein
Farbspiel der Porzellanfliesen
erreicht, die in sieben der acht
Zimmer vorzufinden sind.

De uniformiteit en symmetrie
worden verkregen door het
kleurenspel van de porseleinen
tegels die in zeven van de acht
kamers de vloer bedekken.

La uniformidad y la simetría
se consiguen a partir del juego
cromático de las baldosas de
porcelana colocadas en siete de las
ocho habitaciones.

L'uniformità e la simmetria
si ottengono grazie al gioco
cromatico delle piastrelle di
porcellana collocate in sette delle
otto stanze.

A uniformidade e a simetria
conseguem-se através do jogo de
cores dos azulejos de porcelana
utilizados em sete
das oito divisões.

Enhetlighet och symmetri erhålls
genom en lek med polykroma
porslinsplattor i sju av de åtta
rummen.

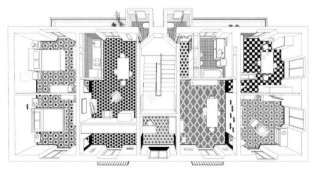

Floor plan in perspective

JAFFA FLAT

PITSOU KEDEM // Tel Aviv, Israel
© Amit Geron

No one knows how many centuries old this Tel Aviv building is, but the aim of the restoration was to reinstate the original style (for example, leaving the vaulted stone roof visible) in combination with a contemporary minimalist language. These two styles go very well together, creating a harmonic and balanced space.

Même si personne ne sait depuis combien de siècles cet édifice de Tel-Aviv existe, l'objectif de la rénovation était de restaurer le style d'origine – en gardant par exemple le plafond voûté en pierre apparent – et de le combiner avec un langage minimaliste contemporain. Les deux styles se marient très bien, créant un espace harmonieux et équilibré.

Man weiß nicht, wie viele hundert Jahre dieses Gebäude in Tel Aviv auf dem Buckel hat, aber Ziel dieser Restauration war die Wiederherstellung des Originalstils (zum Beispiel die Offenlegung der Decke aus Steinbögen) und die Kombination aus zeitgenössischem und minimalistischem Charakter. Beide Stile passen zueinander und schaffen einen harmonischen und ausgeglichenen Raum.

Niemand weet precies hoelang dit pand in Tel Aviv al bestaat, maar het is eeuwenoud. De opzet bij de restauratie was de oorspronkelijke stijl te bewaren (zo bleef bijvoorbeeld het stenen gewelf zichtbaar) en deze te combineren met de eigentijdse minimalistische stijl. Beide stijlen vormen een goed huwelijk en creëren een harmonieuze en evenwichtige ruimte.

No se sabe cuántos cientos de años tiene este edificio de Tel Aviv, pero la intención de la restauración es recuperar el estilo original (por ejemplo, dejando a la vista el techo de piedra abovedado) y combinarlo con un lenguaje minimalista contemporáneo. Ambos estilos casan muy bien, creando un espacio armónico y equilibrado.

No si sa quante centinaia di anni abbia questo edificio di Tel Aviv, ma il fine della ristrutturazione è quello di recuperare lo stile originale (ad esempio, lasciando in vista il soffitto di pietra a volta) e combinarlo con un linguaggio minimalista contemporaneo. I due stili si sposano molto bene, creando uno spazio armonico ed equilibrato.

Não se sabe quantas centenas de anos tem este edifício de Telavive, mas a intenção do restauro era recuperar o estilo original (deixando, por exemplo, à vista o teto de pedra abobadado) e combiná-lo com uma linguagem minimalista contemporânea. Ambos os estilos combinam muito bem, criando um espaço harmonioso e equilibrado.

Ingen vet hur många hundra år gammal denna byggnad i Tel Aviv är, men avsikten med restaureringen var att återfå den ursprungliga stilen (till exempel ta fram det välvda stentaket) och kombinera den med ett modernt minimalistiskt formspråk. De båda stilarna går mycket bra ihop och skapar en harmonisk och balanserad miljö.

Strike a balance between key pieces and light, maximising exterior views.

Instaurez un équilibre entre les pièces essentielles et la lumière en maximisant les vues sur l'extérieur.

Schaffen Sie die Balance zwischen den essenziellen Stücken und dem Licht, um die Aussicht nach draußen zu ermöglichen.

Zoek het evenwicht tussen enkele elementaire basisstukken en een mooie lichtinval die de aandacht vestigt op het uitzicht buiten.

Logra el balance entre las piezas esenciales y la luz maximizando las vistas hacia el exterior.

Raggiungi l'equilibrio tra le parti essenziali e la luce massimizzando la vista sull'esterno.

Consiga um equilíbrio entre as peças essenciais e a luz, maximizando as vistas para o exterior.

Uppnå balans mellan de viktigaste delarna och ljuset och maximera utsikten utåt.

There is no rulebook on how to create a minimalist home. In this case, the basic principles of simplicity interact in a renovated space.

Il n'existe aucun guide pour créer un habitat minimaliste. Dans ce cas, des principes simples et classiques ont été appliqués à cet espace rénové.

Es gibt keine Bedienungsanleitung für die Schaffung eines minimalistischen Heims. In diesem Fall wurden die Grundprinzipien der Schlichtheit mit einem wiederhergestellten Raum kombiniert.

Er bestaan geen vaste richtlijnen om je huis minimalistisch in te richten. Hier worden de basisprincipes van de eenvoud toegepast in een gerenoveerde ruimte.

No existe un manual para crear un hogar minimalista. En este caso se han combinado los principios básicos de la sencillez con un espacio rehabilitado.

Non esiste un manuale per creare una casa minimalista. In questo caso sono stati combinati i principi de base della semplicità in uno spazio ristrutturato.

Não há nenhum manual que ensine a projetar uma casa minimalista. Neste caso, combinaram-se os princípios básicos da simplicidade com um espaço reabilitado.

Det finns ingen handbok i hur man skapar ett minimalistisk hem. I det här fallet har man kombinerat de grundläggande principerna om enkelhet med en renoverad bostad.

ORANGE GROVE

PUGH & SCARPA // West Hollywood, CA, USA
© Marvin Rand

Though sensitively integrated into its surroundings, this home employs a range of materials different from the neighbouring buildings. The height of the roof allowed spaces to be arranged over two levels that benefit from natural light.

Ce lieu s'intègre dans son environnement avec finesse même si tout un éventail de matériaux différents des édifices environnants a été utilisé. La hauteur sous plafond a permis d'agencer les espaces sur deux niveaux tout en tirant profit de la lumière naturelle.

Das Gebäude dieser Wohnung integriert sich mit viel Sensibilität in seine Umgebung. Trotzdem wurde eine andere Palette an Materialien als in den anliegenden Gebäuden gewählt. Die Höhe des Daches ermöglichte es, die Räume in zwei Ebenen aufzuteilen, die von dem Einfall des Lichts profitieren.

Deze woning is goed aangepast aan de omgeving. Niettemin werden bij de bouw andere materialen gebruikt dan bij de omliggende gebouwen. Door de hoogte van het dak kon een indeling met twee lagen die beide een goede lichtinval krijgen, gemaakt worden.

El edificio de esta vivienda se integra con sensibilidad en el entorno. Sin embargo utiliza una paleta de materiales diferente a la de los edificios circundantes. La altura de la cubierta permitió distribuir los espacios en dos niveles que se benefician de la entrada de luz natural.

L'edificio di questa casa si inserisce con delicatezza nel contesto. Tuttavia, utilizza una gamma di materiali diversa rispetto a quella degli edifici circostanti. L'altezza del tetto ha permesso di distribuire gli spazi su due livelli che traggono vantaggio dall'ingresso di luce naturale.

Esta casa integra-se harmoniosamente no meio envolvente. No entanto, utiliza uma paleta de materiais diferente da dos edifícios circundantes. A altura da cobertura permitiu distribuir os espaços em dois níveis, que beneficiam da entrada da luz natural.

Bostadshuset integrerades med stor medvetenhet med omgivningen. Ändå användes en mängd olika material som skiljer sig från de omgivande byggnaderna. Höjden gjorde att man kunde fördela rummen på två våningar vilket underlättade insläppet av dagsljus.

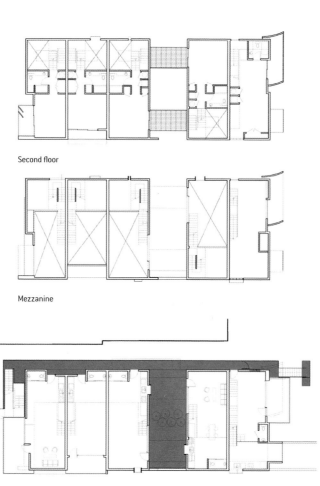

Second floor

Mezzanine

Ground floor

Conventional features such
as windows and porches were
thought as an abstract sculptural
ensemble, which is typical in
minimalism.

Les éléments conventionnels,
comme les fenêtres et les
porches, ont été conçus comme
un ensemble sculptural abstrait,
caractéristique des structures
minimalistes.

Die konventionellen Elemente,
wie Fenster und Vorhalle, wurden
als ein bildhauerisches Konstrukt
aufgefasst, das minimalistische
Strukturen aufweist.

Gebruikelijke elementen zoals
ramen en portalen zijn hier
als een abstract, plastisch
geheel ontworpen, eigen aan
minimalistische structuren.

Los elementos convencionales,
como las ventanas y los porches,
se concibieron como un conjunto
escultórico abstracto, propio de
estructuras minimalistas.

Gli elementi convenzionali,
come le finestre e i portici, sono
stati concepiti come un insieme
scultoreo astratto, tipico delle
strutture minimaliste.

Os elementos convencionais, como
as janelas e os pórticos, foram
concebidos como um conjunto
escultórico abstrato, característico
das estruturas minimalistas.

Konventionella element,
som fönster och verandor,
har här setts som en samling
abstrakta skulpturer, enligt den
minimalistiska grundtanken.

Ensure that natural lighting prevails over artificial. Double-height spaces have the advantage of allowing light to spread vertically.

Il faut faire en sorte que la lumière naturelle prévale sur l'artificielle. Les espaces présentant une double hauteur avec fenêtres profitent d'une distribution verticale de la lumière.

Das natürliche Sonnenlicht soll über dem künstlichen Licht stehen. Die Räume doppelter Höhe ermöglichen es, dass man von Vorteilen in der vertikalen Raumaufteilung profitieren kann.

Natuurlijk licht is altijd te verkiezen boven artificieel licht. Doordat de ruimtes uit twee lagen bestaan, kunnen ze zo veel mogelijk voordeel halen uit de verticale indeling.

Hay que procurar que la iluminación natural prevalezca sobre la artificial. Los espacios de doble altura permiten beneficiarse de las ventajas de la distribución vertical.

Bisogna fare in modo che l'illuminazione naturale prevalga su quella artificiale. Gli spazi a doppia altezza consentono di godere dei vantaggi della distribuzione verticale.

É importante que a iluminação natural se sobreponha à artificial. Os espaços com duplo pé-direito permitem tirar partido das vantagens da distribuição vertical.

Man måste se till att det naturliga ljuset får huvudrollen framför det konstgjorda. Rum med dubbel takhöjd kan dra nytta av höga fönster.

SHIMOSAKUNOBE K

RICO TURU ARCHITECTS STUDIO // Kawasaki, Kanagawa, Japan
© Koji Okumura

This project covers four levels and functions as both home and office. A staircase in the main entrance leads to the living area and kitchen on the fourth floor, which acts as an observation deck. The simplicity of the design allows the countryside to become the main visual attraction.

Ce projet s'étend sur quatre niveaux et combine les fonctions de bureau et d'espace de vie. Un escalier au niveau de l'entrée principale mène au salon et à la cuisine situés au quatrième étage, qui sert de belvédère. Grâce à une esthétique simple, c'est le paysage qui devient la principale attraction visuelle.

Dieses Projekt wird auf vier Ebenen ausgeführt und hat die Funktionen einer Wohnung und eines Büros. Eine Treppe am Haupteingang führt ins Wohnzimmer und in die Küche, die sich im vierten Stockwerk befinden, das als Aussichtspunkt dient. Die Schlichtheit der Ästhetik ermöglicht es, dass sich die Landschaft in die visuelle Hauptattraktion verwandelt.

Dit project is gerealiseerd in vier lagen en biedt onderdak aan zowel woon- als kantoorruimte. Een trap bij de hoofdingang leidt naar de leefruimte en de keuken die op de vierde etage gebouwd zijn als een veranda met uitzicht. Door de esthetische eenvoud trekt vooral de natuurlijke omgeving de aandacht.

Este proyecto se desarrolla en cuatro niveles y acoge las funciones de vivienda y oficina. Una escalera en la entrada principal conduce hasta la zona de estar y la cocina situadas en la cuarta planta, que actúa de mirador. La simplicidad de la estética permite que el paisaje se convierta en la principal atracción visual.

Questo progetto si sviluppa su quattro livelli e comprende le funzioni di abitazione e ufficio. Una scala all'ingresso principale conduce verso il soggiorno e la cucina situati al quarto piano, che viene utilizzato come veranda. La semplicità dell'estetica consente al paesaggio di diventare la principale attrattiva visiva.

Este projeto desenvolve-se em quatro níveis e destina-se às funções de habitação e escritório. A escada que parte da entrada principal conduz à zona de estar e à cozinha, situadas no último andar, que funciona como mirante. A simplicidade da estética faz com que a paisagem se torne o principal elemento de atração visual.

Projektet är uppdelat på fyra våningar och fungerar som bostad och kontor. En trappa från huvudentrén leder till vardagsrum och kök som ligger på fjärde våningen, som också är en utkikspunkt. Enkelheten i utseendet gör att landskapet att bli den viktigaste visuella attraktionen.

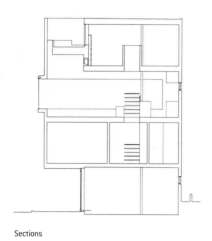
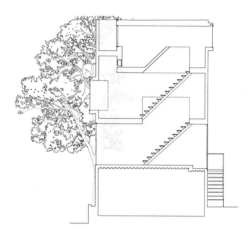

Sections

The intention with this plan was to incorporate a feature into the construction that would act as a connection with the outside world.

Le but de ce projet a été d'intégrer, au moment de la construction, un élément servant de lien avec l'extérieur.

Ziel dieses Projektes war es, in die Konstruktion ein Element mit einfließen zu lassen, das die Verbindung nach draußen gewährt.

De opzet van dit project was om in de constructie een element te laten integreren met het exterieur.

La intención de este proyecto fue integrar en la construcción un elemento que actuara de conexión con el exterior.

Il fine di questo progetto era integrare nella costruzione un elemento che fungesse da collegamento con l'esterno.

A intenção deste projeto foi integrar na construção um elemento que funcionasse como ponte de ligação ao exterior.

Avsikten med projektet var att integrera ett element i byggnaden som kopplar samman utsidan med insidan.

An elongated window acts as a screen and invites you to discover the outside.

Une baie vitrée élargie se déploie le long du volume, semblable à un écran invitant à découvrir l'extérieur.

Ein längliches Fenster wird vollständig geöffnet und dient als Bildschirm, der dazu einlädt, den Außenbereich zu erkunden.

Een groot hoog raam dient als wandscherm en nodigt uit om de omgeving buiten te verkennen.

Un ventanal alargado se despliega a lo largo del volumen actuando de pantalla e invita a descubrir el exterior.

Un finestrone allungato si distende per tutto il volume rivestendo la funzione di schermo e invita a scoprire l'esterno.

O janelão alongado que percorre todo o volume funciona como um ecrã e convida à descoberta do exterior.

Ett avlångt fönster sträcker sig längs hela väggen och fungerar som ett skyltfönster som bjuder in till att upptäcka insidan.

Third floor

Second floor

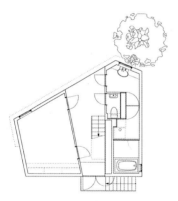

First floor

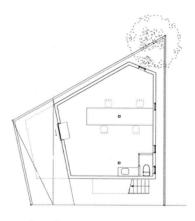

Ground floor

HOUSE IN BERA

JABIER LEKUONA , XABIER ARRUABARRENA, JULEN LEKUONA // Bera, Spain
© Gogortza & Llorella

This home was designed for the needs of its disabled owner. Its mainly open plan allows as much freedom of movement as possible, with few features that would hinder a wheelchair.

Cette maison a été conçue pour répondre aux besoins spécifiques de son propriétaire souffrant d'un handicap. Un agencement ouvert prévalait afin d'obtenir une grande liberté de mouvement, avec peu d'éléments pour ne pas entraver le déplacement d'un fauteuil roulant.

Diese Wohnung wurde entworfen, um den speziellen Bedürfnissen eines behinderten Besitzers gerecht zu werden. Er bevorzugte eine offene Raumverteilung, um so viel Bewegungsfreiheit wie möglich zu erschaffen, mit wenigen Elementen, die die Umstellung in einem Rollstuhl erschweren würde.

De eigenaar heeft een handicap en daarom is deze woning ontworpen op basis van zijn specifieke behoeften. Bij de indeling werd gekozen voor open ruimtes met weinig elementen om in een rolstoel zo veel mogelijk vrij en zonder belemmeringen te kunnen bewegen.

Esta vivienda fue diseñada para responder a las necesidades específicas de su propietario discapacitado. Prevaleció una distribución abierta que permitiera la mayor libertad de movimientos posible, con pocos elementos que puedan entorpecer el desplazamiento en silla de ruedas.

Questa casa è stata progettata per andare incontro alle esigenze specifiche che il suo proprietario disabile necessitava. È prevalsa una distribuzione aperta che consentisse la maggiore libertà di movimento possibile, con pochi elementi che ostacolassero lo spostamento in sedia a rotelle.

Esta casa foi desenhada para dar resposta às necessidades específicas do proprietário, portador de deficiência. Optou-se por uma distribuição aberta do espaço, que permitisse a maior liberdade de movimentos possível, evitando elementos que pudessem dificultar a deslocação em cadeira de rodas.

Den här bostaden har utformats för att möta den handikappade ägarens specifika behov. Här råder en öppen planlösning som ger största möjliga rörelsefrihet, med få inslag som är i vägen för en rullstol.

The transparent facade on one side creates a dialogue between the constructed block and its open counterpart.

Le bloc établit un dialogue avec l'extérieur où il se prolonge grâce à une façade transparente sur l'un des côtés.

Der konstruierte Block steht durch eine durchsichtige Fassade an einer seiner Seiten in Verbindung zu seinem offenen Gegenstück.

Dit blok staat in verbinding met een ander blok dat open kan via de transparante zijwand.

El bloque construido dialoga con su contraparte abierta a través de una fachada transparente en uno de sus lados.

Il blocco costruito dialoga con la sua controparte aperta attraverso una facciata trasparente su uno dei suoi lati.

O bloco construído dialoga com o seu homólogo aberto através de uma fachada transparente num dos lados.

Blockhuset sammanförs med omgivningen genom en transparent fasad på en av sidorna.

Elevation

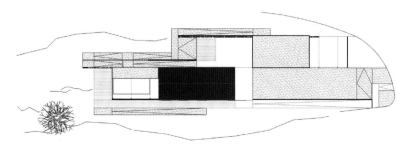

Roof plan

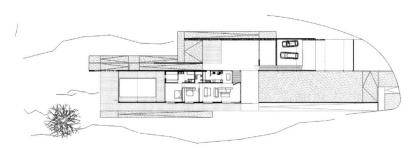

Floor plan

Elevation

The concept for this dwelling is based on the idea of positive and negative space, opening and closing the spaces to the outside.

Cette pièce se base sur un concept d'espace positif et négatif, à la fois ouvert et fermé, un intérieur donnant sur l'extérieur.

Das Konzept dieses Wohnraumes beruht auf der Idee von einem positiven und einem negativen Raum, der die Fläche nach außen öffnet und schließt.

Deze woning is geconcipieerd met het idee dat ruimtes elkaars tegenpolen zijn en dat ze zich van het exterieur kunnen afsluiten of er juist voor open kunnen staan.

El concepto de esta vivienda se basa en la idea de espacio positivo y negativo, abriendo y cerrando los espacios hacia el exterior.

L'idea di questa casa si basa sul concetto di spazio positivo e negativo, aprendo e chiudendo gli spazi sull'esterno.

O conceito desta casa baseia-se na ideia de espaço positivo e negativo, abrindo e fechando os espaços ao exterior.

Konceptet bakom det här huset är baserat på idén om positiv och negativ rymd, som öppnar och stänger utrymmen i förhållande till omvärlden.

M LIDIA HOUSE

RCR ARQUITECTES // Montagut, Spain
© Hisao Suzuki

A prefabricated construction of two separate sections separated by a glazed space compose this home. The structure is notable for the simplicity of its materials, with metal panels at the ends complementing the glazed surfaces in the middle section.

Cette maison est basée sur une construction préfabriquée qui comporte deux sections séparées par un volume vitré. La structure se démarque par la simplicité des matériaux utilisés – avec des panneaux métalliques aux extrémités – et les surfaces vitrées du volume intermédiaire.

Diese Wohnung beruht auf einer vorgefertigten Konstruktion, die aus zwei Abschnitten besteht, die durch einen gläsernes Element getrennt werden. Die Struktur sticht aufgrund ihrer schlichten Materialien hervor, mit Metallpaneelen an den jeweiligen Enden, sowie durch die verglasten Oberflächen des Zwischenstücks.

Deze woning is een prefabconstructie die bestaat uit twee aparte secties met een glazen verbinding. De structuur valt op door haar eenvoud aan gebruikte materialen, met metalen platen op de uiteinden en glas voor het middenstuk.

Esta vivienda se basa en una construcción prefabricada compuesta por dos secciones separadas por un volumen acristalado. La estructura destaca por la sencillez de los materiales, con paneles de metal en los extremos, y por las superficies acristaladas del volumen intermedio.

Questa abitazione si basa su di una costruzione prefabbricata composta di due sezioni separate da un volume a vetri. La struttura spicca per la semplicità dei materiali, con pannelli di metallo alle estremità, e per le superfici a vetri del volume intermedio.

Esta casa tem por base uma construção prefabricada, constituída por duas secções separadas por um volume envidraçado. A estrutura destaca-se pela simplicidade dos materiais, com painéis de metal nas extremidades, e pelas superfícies envidraçadas do volume intermédio.

Den här bostaden grundar sig på en prefabricerad byggnad bestående av två sektioner åtskilda av en glasdel. Strukturen utmärker sig genom de enkla materialen, med metallpaneler på ändarna och glasytor i mellandelen.

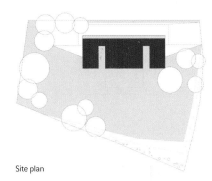

Site plan

The interiors of the solid volumes at the ends are not visible from neighbouring properties; these are the private areas.

Les volumes solides aux extrémités préservent de la curiosité des voisins et apportent de l'intimité à ces espaces.

Der solide Rauminhalt der Extreme bleibt optisch vor den Nachbarn verschlossen und bringt Privatsphäre.

De stevige blokken aan beide uiteinden bieden privacy en liggen uit het zicht van de buren.

Los volúmenes sólidos de los extremos quedan cerrados a la visibilidad de los vecinos y dan privacidad a estas áreas.

I volumi solidi delle estremità risultano chiusi alla vista dei vicini e attribuiscono intimità a queste aree.

Os volumes sólidos das extremidades ficam fora do ângulo de visão dos vizinhos, conferindo privacidade a estas áreas.

Solida väggar åt sidorna skiljer av insynen från grannarna och ger avskildhet i bostaden.

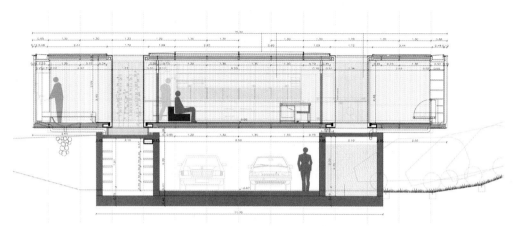

Longitudinal section

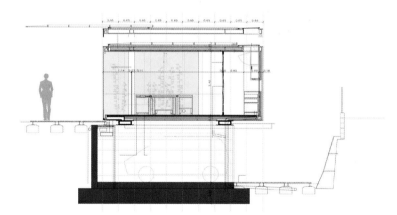

Transversal section

Glazed dividing walls achieve a sense of depth and height and create rhythm by breaking up the continuous horizontal alignment of the space.

Intercalez des cloisons en verre. Vous obtiendrez une impression de profondeur et de hauteur, mais aussi un rythme en brisant l'horizontalité continue de l'espace.

Bauen Sie kristallisierte Trennwände ein. Sie werden das Gefühl von Raumtiefe und Höhe bekommen und durch die Abschaffung der Horizontalität des Raumes Rhythmus schaffen.

Plaats glazen tussenwanden. Zo creëer je een gevoel van diepte en hoogte en breek je de horizontale, doorlopende lijn van de ruimte.

Intercala muros divisorios acristalados. Lograrás un sentido de profundidad y altura, y crearás ritmo al romper con la horizontalidad continua del espacio.

Inserisci muri divisori a vetri. Otterrai un senso di profondità e altezza, e genererai ritmo interrompendo l'orizzontalità continua dello spazio.

Intercale paredes divisórias envidraçadas. Ao romper com a horizontalidade contínua do espaço, consegue uma sensação de profundidade e altura.

Foga in mellanväggar av glas. Du kommer att uppnå en känsla av djup och höjd, och får en rytm som bryter av från det kontinuerliga horisontella utrymmet.

HILL SIDE HOUSE

HAYBALL LEONARD STENT, SUE CARR // Melbourne, Australia
© Courtesy of Hayball Leonard Stent, Sue Carr

The designers of this house wanted to create a spacious interior open to the outside, and to avoid unnecessary enclosures that would impede communication between the different spaces. Communal areas such as the kitchen, lounge, and dining room share the same perimeter.

L'objectif principal au moment de concevoir l'intérieur de cette maison était d'obtenir une zone large et ouverte sur l'extérieur ne présentant aucun cloisonnement superflu pour éviter d'entraver la communication entre les différents lieux. Les parties communes, comme la cuisine, le salon et la salle à manger, partagent le même périmètre.

Das Hauptziel zum Zeitpunkt des Innendesigns dieser Wohnung war es, eine weite und offene Fläche nach draußen zu schaffen, die unnötige Einschließungen verhindern und die Verbindung der verschiedenen Räume behindern würde. Die öffentlichen Räume, wie Badezimmer, Wohn- und Esszimmer, haben denselben Umfang.

De belangrijkste doelstelling bij het ontwerp van deze woning was een brede en open zone naar buiten toe creëren, zonder onnodige belemmeringen voor de communicatie tussen de interieur en exterieur. De leefruimtes, waaronder de keuken, de salon en de eetkamer beslaan één grote ruimte.

El principal objetivo a la hora de diseñar el interior de esta vivienda fue conseguir una zona amplia y abierta al exterior que evitara cerramientos innecesarios que entorpecieran la comunicación de los diferentes ámbitos. Las zonas comunes, como la cocina, el salón y el comedor, comparten el mismo perímetro.

L'obiettivo principale quando è stato progettato l'interno di questa casa è stato ottenere una zona ampia e aperta all'esterno che evitasse chiusure superflue che potessero intralciare la comunicazione fra i vari ambienti. Le zone comuni, come la cucina, il salotto e la sala da pranzo, condividono lo stesso perimetro.

O principal objetivo para o projeto do interior desta casa foi conseguir uma zona ampla e aberta para o exterior, evitando divisórias desnecessárias que impedissem a comunicação entre as várias áreas. As áreas comuns, como a cozinha, a sala e a sala de jantar, partilham o mesmo espaço.

Det viktigaste när detta hus inredning ritades var att åstadkomma en stor och öppen del som vette mot utsidan för att undvika onödiga begränsningar och för att öppna för kommunikation åt båda hållen. De gemensamma delarna, som kök, vardagsrum och matsal, samsas i samma utrymme.

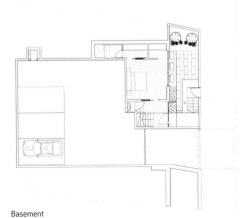

Basement

First floor

If possible, create a single free space for the public area. Consider creating different configurations with pivoting walls.

Si le lieu s'y prête, optez pour la création d'un seul espace libre en guise de zone publique, sans écarter la possibilité d'aménager l'espace de différentes façons grâce à des murs pivotants.

Wenn es der Platz ermöglicht, schaffen Sie einen einzigen freien Raum als öffentlichen Bereich. Schließen Sie die Möglichkeit nicht aus, verschiedene Gestaltungsmodelle mit drehenden Mauern zu schaffen.

Als de ruimte het toelaat, creëer dan één vrije ruimte die gemeenschappelijk is. Een optie is om deze ruimte naar behoefte in te delen met draaiende wanden.

Si el lugar te lo permite, opta por crear un solo espacio libre para el área pública. No descartes la posibilidad de establecer diferentes configuraciones con muros pivotantes.

Se il luogo lo consente, opta per creare un unico spazio libero per l'area pubblica. Non scartare la possibilità di stabilire diverse configurazioni con muri pivotanti.

Se o local o permitir, opte por criar um espaço único para as áreas sociais. Não descarte a possibilidade de flexibilizar a configuração do espaço através de paredes giratórias.

Om utrymmet tillåter det kan du skapa ett enda rum som rymmer alla de allmänna funktionerna. Uteslut inte möjligheten att skapa olika konfigurationer med svängbara väggar.

Second floor

Choose a subtle, restful design for the bedroom. Compositional purity and neutral tones are recommended for alleviating fatigue.

Optez pour une chambre épurée pour en faire un réel espace de détente. Combinez une composition pure et des tons neutres qui sont les plus indiqués pour se délasser.

Entscheiden Sie sich für ein weniger auffälliges Schlafzimmer, damit der Entspannungseffekt nicht ausbleibt. Wählen Sie eine kompositorische Reinheit und neutrale Töne, die am besten eine Übersättigung verhindern.

Ga voor een sober ingerichte slaapkamer waar je goed kunt ontspannen. Kies voor een zuivere compositie en neutrale tonen die zorgen voor een goede nachtrust.

Decántate por un dormitorio poco llamativo, que no altere el relax. Opta por la pureza compositiva y los tonos neutros, que son los más indicados para mitigar la fatiga.

Propendi per una stanza da letto poco appariscente, che non alteri il relax. Opta per la purezza compositiva e i toni neutri, che sono i più indicati per attenuare la fatica.

Prefira um quarto pouco chamativo, que não perturbe o relaxamento. Opte pela pureza da composição e pelos tons neutros, que são os mais indicados para aliviar o cansaço.

Välj ett sovrum som är diskret och inte stör avkopplingen. Satsa på en ren sammansättning och neutrala toner, som är bäst lämpade för att avhjälpa tröttheten.

PAVI HOUSE

JOHANNES KAUFMANN ARCHITEKTUR // Bad Waltersdorf, Austria
© Courtesy of Johannes Kaufmann Architektur

Pavi House could be considered a modern interpretation of an Austrian mountain hut. The combination of wood and large windows confers an austere and elegant aesthetic that contrasts with the stone floor and white furniture.

Pavi House peut être considérée comme une interprétation moderne des chalets de montagne autrichiens. La combinaison du bois avec de grandes ouvertures vitrées lui confère une esthétique dépouillée et élégante qui contraste avec le sol en pierre et le mobilier blanc.

Pavi House kann als eine moderne Interpretation von Wohnungen in den österreichischen Bergen gesehen werden. Die Kombination aus Holz mit großen verglasten Öffnungen verleiht eine nüchterne und elegante Ästhetik, die mit dem Steinboden und weißen Möbeln im Kontrast steht.

Pavi House kan gezien worden als een moderne interpretatie van het Oostenrijkse chalet. Door het gebruik van hout gecombineerd met grote glazen oppervlaktes krijgt het huis een sobere maar elegante uitstraling die contrasteert met de stenen vloer en het witte meubilair.

Pavi House se puede considerar una interpretación moderna de las viviendas de montaña austríacas. La combinación de madera con grandes aperturas acristaladas le confiere una estética austera y elegante que contrasta con el suelo de piedra y el mobiliario blanco.

Pavi House può essere considerata un'interpretazione moderna delle case di montagna austriache. La combinazione del legno con grandi aperture a vetri le conferisce un'estetica austera ed elegante che contrasta con il pavimento in pietra e i mobili bianchi.

A Pavi House pode ser considerada como uma interpretação moderna das casas de montanha austríacas. A combinação da madeira com grandes aberturas envidraçadas confere-lhe uma estética austera e elegante, que contrasta com o chão de pedra e o mobiliário branco.

Pavi House kan ses som en modern tolkning av de österrikiska alpstugorna. Kombinationen av trä med stora inglasade delar ger ett stramt och elegant utseende som kontrasterar mot stengolvet och de vita möblerna.

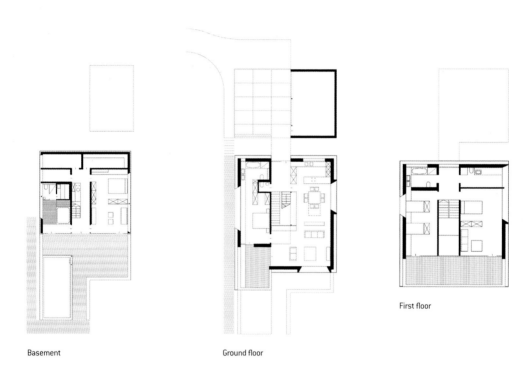

Basement

Ground floor

First floor

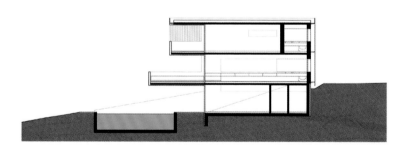

Section

Optimize the space below the staircase. This is a practical and decorative way to organize things that would otherwise take up valuable space.

Exploitez l'espace sous l'escalier. Vous arriverez à organiser de façon pratique et décorative des éléments qui, sans cela, occuperaient probablement un espace précieux.

Optimieren Sie den Raum unterhalb der Treppe. Sie werden Elemente auf praktische und dekorative Art organisieren können, die sonst den so wertvollen Raum einnehmen.

Maak gebruik van de ruimte onder de trap. Zo kun je op een praktische manier mooie, decoratieve elementen plaatsen die anders kostbare ruimte zouden innemen.

Optimiza el espacio que queda debajo de la escalera. Conseguirás organizar de forma práctica y decorativa elementos que de otra forma ocuparían un lugar valioso.

Ottimizza lo spazio sottostante la scala. Riuscirai a organizzare in modo pratico e decorativo elementi che altrimenti occuperebbero uno spazio prezioso.

Otimize o vão da escada. Vai, assim, conseguir organizar de forma prática e decorativa elementos que, de outro modo, iriam ocupar um espaço valioso.

Ta vara på utrymmet under trappan. Du kan organisera det till något praktiskt och dekorativt, i stället för att bara ta upp värdefull plats.

Create transparent spaces using light textures and materials. This will create a constant dialogue with the exterior.

Générez des espaces transparents avec des textures et des matériaux légers afin de créer un dialogue ininterrompu avec l'extérieur.

Schaffen Sie transparente Räume mit Struktur und leichten Materialien. Sie erreichen die dauerhafte Verbindung mit dem Außenbereich.

Creëer transparante ruimtes door lichte materialen en texturen te gebruiken die communiceren met de buitenwereld.

Genera espacios transparentes con texturas y materiales livianos. Crearás un diálogo constante con el exterior.

Genera spazi trasparenti con trame e materiali leggeri. Darai vita a un dialogo costante con l'esterno.

Crie espaços transparentes com texturas e materiais diáfanos. Vai criar um diálogo constante com o exterior.

Skapa transparenta ytor med lätta texturer och material. Du kommer att skapa en kontinuerlig dialog med utsidan.

CC_01 HOUSE

LEVEN BETTS STUDIO // Columbia County, NY, USA
© Courtesy of Leven Betts Studio

This house consists of two diagonally arranged volumes that stretch across the landscape without aesthetic pretensions. The two volumes, characterised by the simplicity of their forms, create an interesting minimalist atmosphere dominated by glass, PVC, and aluminium.

Cette maison comporte deux volumes en diagonale qui s'étendent sur le paysage. Leur tracé ne révèle aucune prétention esthétique. Et pourtant, ces deux éléments, qui se caractérisent par la simplicité de leurs formes, abritent une atmosphère minimaliste intéressante où se démarquent des matériaux comme le verre, le PVC et l'aluminium.

Diese Wohnung setzt sich aus zwei diagonalen Körpern zusammen, die sich in ihrem Entwurf ohne ästhetische Ansprüche über die Landschaft ziehen. Die zwei Gebilde, die sich durch ihre einfachen Formen auszeichnen, verbergen in ihrem Inneren eine interessante und minimalistische Atmosphäre, in der Materialien wie Glas, PVC und Aluminium hervorstechen.

Het ontwerp van dit huis zonder esthetische pretenties bestaat uit twee diagonale delen die zich uitstrekken in het omliggende landschap. Binnenin creëren de twee eenvoudige blokken een aangename, minimalistische sfeer waarbij vooral het gebruik van glas, PVC en aluminium opvallen.

Esta vivienda se compone de dos cuerpos en diagonal que se extienden sobre el paisaje sin pretensiones estéticas en su trazado. Los dos volúmenes, caracterizados por la simplicidad de sus formas, albergan en su interior una interesante atmósfera minimalista en la que destacan materiales como el cristal, el PVC y el aluminio.

Questa casa è composta di due corpi in diagonale che si estendono sul paesaggio senza pretese estetiche nel loro percorso. I due volumi, caratterizzati dalla semplicità delle forme, racchiudono al loro interno un'interessante atmosfera minimalista in cui spiccano materiali come il vetro, il PVC e l'alluminio.

Esta casa é constituída por dois corpos em diagonal, que se estendem pela paisagem sem pretensões estéticas no seu traçado. Os dois volumes, caracterizados pela simplicidade das suas formas, encerram no interior uma interessante atmosfera minimalista, em que se destacam materiais como o vidro, o PVC e o alumínio.

Den här bostaden består av två diagonala sektioner som sträcker sig över landskapet utan estetiska pretentioner. De två sektionerna, som kännetecknas av sina enkla former, har en intressant minimalistisk atmosfär med framträdande material som glas, PVC och aluminium.

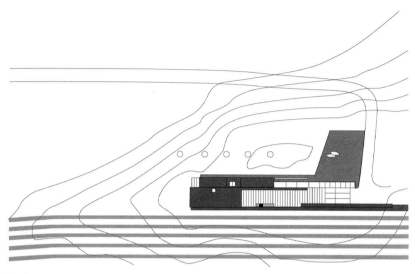

Site plan

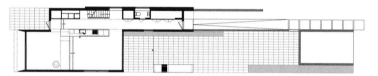

First floor

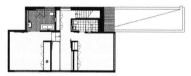

Ground floor

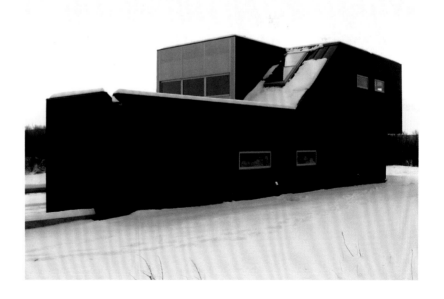

HOUSE Nº5

CLAESSON KOIVISTO RUNE ARCHITECTS // Nacka, Sweden
© Courtesy of Claesson Koivisto Rune Architects

A graphic designer, the owner of this property commissioned a home that would reflect his taste for geometrical aesthetics and formal proportions. Inside, the decor is contained; mostly natural materials such as wood were used. The only element that stands out is the black cast-iron fireplace at the back of the room.

Le propriétaire de cette maison, un concepteur graphique de métier, s'est lancé dans la réalisation d'une maison qui reflèterait son goût pour l'esthétique géométrique et la proportion des formes. À l'intérieur, la décoration est sommaire et l'usage de matériaux naturels comme le bois prédomine. Seule se démarque la cheminée noire en fer forgé au fond du salon.

Der Besitzer dieser Wohnung, ein Grafikdesigner, gab eine Wohnung in Auftrag, die seinen Geschmack für die geometrische Ästhetik und die Proportion der Formen widerspiegelt. Im Inneren ist die Dekoration eher gemäßigt und es dominiert der Gebrauch von natürlichen Materialien wie Holz. Es sticht lediglich der schwarze Schornstein aus Schmelzeisen im hinteren Teil des Salons hervor.

De eigenaar van deze woning is grafisch ontwerper. Het ontwerp weerspiegelt zijn voorkeur voor een geometrische vormgeving met goede proporties. Het interieur is ingetogen en er is gebruik gemaakt van natuurlijke materialen zoals hout. Alleen de zwarte gietijzeren schoorsteenpijp neemt een prominente plaats in tegen de achterwand van de salon.

El propietario de esta vivienda, diseñador gráfico de profesión, encargó una vivienda que reflejara su gusto por la estética geométrica y la proporción de las formas. En el interior, la decoración es contenida y predomina el uso de materiales naturales como la madera. Solo destaca la chimenea negra de hierro fundido, al fondo del salón.

Il proprietario di questa casa, disegnatore grafico di professione, ha richiesto una casa che rispecchiasse il suo gusto per l'estetica geometrica e la proporzione delle forme. All'interno, la decorazione è contenuta e predomina l'utilizzo di materiali naturali come il legno. Si distingue solo il caminetto nero di ghisa, in fondo al salone.

O proprietário desta casa, *designer* gráfico de profissão, encomendou um projeto que refletisse o seu gosto pela estética geométrica e a proporção das formas. No interior, a decoração é contida e predomina o uso de materiais naturais como a madeira. Em grande destaque, a lareira negra de ferro fundido, ao fundo da sala.

Denna bostads ägare, som är grafisk formgivare till yrket, beställde ett hem som avspeglade hans smak för geometri och proportionella former. Inuti är inredningen dämpad och det som dominerar är användningen av naturmaterial som trä. Det enda som framträder är den svarta gjutjärnsspisen, längst in i vardagsrummet.

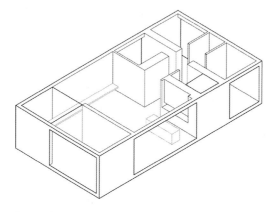

Axonometric

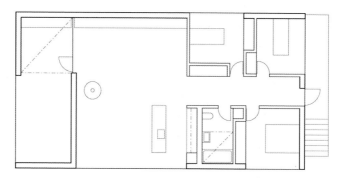

Floor plan

TREGUNTER

davidclovers // Hong Kong, China
© davidclovers (assisted by Ziyin Zhou)

With unique views of Victoria Harbour, this building rises from Hong Kong's forest of skyscrapers. The roof is corrugated to make it look like it contracts and expands. The use of wood and plaster and the mosaic tiles in the bathrooms enhance the lighting and make for a truly minimalist space.

Dans la forêt de tours de Hong Kong s'élève cet édifice aux vues uniques sur le port de Victoria. Le plafond est ondulé et semble se compresser et s'élargir. La combinaison harmonieuse de bois et de plâtre ainsi que la mosaïque de carreaux des salles de bains renforcent l'éclairage et font de ce lieu un véritable espace minimaliste.

In der Turmlandschaft von Hong Kong steht dieses Gebäude mit einzigartigen Ausblicken auf den Victoria Hafen. Das Dach des Hauses ist gewölbt und erweckt den Anschein, dass es sich zusammenzieht und wieder expandiert. Die minimale Verwendung von Holz, Gips und Mosaik in den Badfliesen verstärkt die Beleuchtung und verwandelt den Turm wahrlich in einen minimalistischen Ort.

Tussen de wolkenkrabbers van Hong Kong staat deze toren met uniek uitzicht over de Victoria haven. Het plafond is golvend en lijkt in te krimpen en uit te zetten. Het minimale gebruik van hout en gips en de oplichtende mozaïeksteentjes in de badkamers maken van deze toren een echt minimalistische ruimte.

Entre el bosque de torres de Hong Kong se alza esta, con unas vistas únicas del puerto de Victoria. El techo de la casa es ondulado para que parezca que se comprime y se expande. El uso mínimo de la madera y del yeso y el mosaico de azulejos de los baños potencian la iluminación y hacen de la torre un verdadero espacio minimalista.

Nella foresta di torri di Hong Kong si erge questa, con una vista unica sul porto di Victoria. Il tetto della casa è ondulato in modo che sembra comprimersi ed espandersi. L'utilizzo minimo del legno e del gesso e il mosaico di piastrelle dei bagni potenziano l'illuminazione e fanno della torre un autentico spazio minimalista.

Por entre a floresta de torres de Hong Kong, ergue-se esta, com vistas únicas sobre o porto de Victoria. O telhado da casa é ondulado, para dar a impressão de que se comprime e se expande. O uso parcimonioso da madeira e do reboco e o mosaico de azulejos das casas de banho potenciam a iluminação e fazem desta torre um verdadeiro espaço minimalista.

Bland skogen av skyskrapor i Hongkong hittar vi detta hus, med unik utsikt över Victoria-hamnen. Husets tak är vågformat för att ge intryck av att utrymmet växer eller krymper. Den minimala användningen av trä och gips och mosaiken i badrummen förbättrar belysningen och gör våningen verkligt minimalistisk.

Minimalist spaces can be colourful when saturated rugs or chairs are set against austerity and geometry in a balanced way.

Il existe des ambiances dites minimalistes coloristes où des tapis et des chaises de couleur se conjuguent avec l'austérité et la géométrie en toute harmonie.

Es gibt Vorschläge zu minimalistisch bunten Räumen, in denen die farbenfrohen Teppiche oder Stühle die Nüchternheit und Geometrie auf eine ausgeglichene Art und Weise miteinander verbinden.

Minimalistisch design kan ook kleur bekennen betekenen in de keuze voor tapijten of in de aankleding van stoelen, tegenover een sobere, geometrische en evenwichtige vormgeving.

Existen propuestas de ambientes minimalistas coloristas en los que las alfombras o las sillas coloridas conjugan con la austeridad y la geometría de una forma equilibrada.

Esistono proposte di ambienti minimalisti coloristi in cui i tappeti e le sedie colorate si coniugano con l'austerità e la geometria in modo equilibrato.

Existem propostas de ambientes minimalistas coloristas, que combinam alcatifas ou cadeiras coloridas com a austeridade e a geometria de uma forma equilibrada.

Det finns förslag på minimalistiska men färgglada miljöer där färgglada mattor eller stolar i kombination med stramhet och geometriska former ger balans.

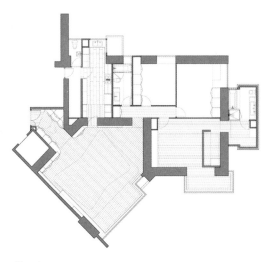

Floor plan

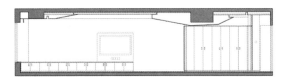

Section through entry and living room

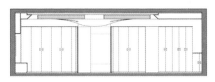

Section of the living room

Minimalist kitchens stand out, above all, for their linear simplicity and order.

Les cuisines minimalistes se démarquent surtout par la simplicité de leurs lignes et l'ordre qui y règne.

Die minimalistischen Küchen stechen hauptsächlich durch die Schlichtheit Ihrer Linien und ihre Ordnung hervor.

Wat een minimalistische keuken kenmerkt zijn orde en eenvoudige lijnen.

Las cocinas minimalistas destacan sobre todo por la sencillez de sus líneas y por su orden.

Le cucine minimaliste spiccano soprattutto per la semplicità delle loro linee e per il loro ordine.

As cozinhas minimalistas caracterizam-se sobretudo pela simplicidade das suas linhas e pela sua organização.

Det minimalistiska köket utmärker sig framför allt genom enkelheten i linjerna och genom ordningen.

SLIP HOUSE

CARL TURNER ARCHITECTS // Brixton, United Kingdom
© Tim Crocker

This house was designed as a home for the architect himself, who particularly wanted it to be both ecologically and financially sustainable. Its structural simplicity enhances its adaptability. It consists of three overlapping cubes that maximise natural light penetration and can be adapted to different uses in the future.

Cette maison a été conçue comme un foyer pour l'architecte en personne, qui a tout particulièrement cherché à obtenir un habitat aussi écologique qu'économique. La simplicité de la structure, qui est composée de trois cubes superposés, offre une entrée de lumière maximale et valorise la flexibilité du lieu qu'elle rend modulable pour des usages futurs.

Dieses Haus wurde als Unterkunft für den Architekten selbst entworfen, der besonders Wert darauf legte, dass es beständig, umweltfreundlich und preiswert ist. Die Schlichtheit der Struktur, die aus drei aufeinander liegenden Würfeln besteht, die den Einfall des Lichts bestärken, erhöht die Flexibilität des Hauses und passt es an die Zukunft an.

Dit huis is ontworpen als eigen woning voor de architect die het belangrijk vond dat het huis zowel ecologisch als economisch duurzaam zou zijn. De eenvoudige structuur bestaat uit drie op elkaar gestapelde kubusvormige blokken. Er is maximale lichtinval en de vorm van het huis maakt het flexibel en geschikt voor andere toekomstige functies.

Esta casa fue diseñada como hogar para el propio arquitecto, que tuvo especialmente en cuenta que fuera sostenible tanto ecológica como económicamente. La sencillez de la estructura, que está formada por tres cubos superpuestos que maximizan la entrada de luz, potencia la flexibilidad de la casa y la hace adaptable a usos futuros.

Questa casa è stata progettata come abitazione dello stesso architetto, che ha dato particolare importanza al fatto che fosse sostenibile sia dal punto di vista ecologico, sia economico. La semplicità della struttura, formata da tre cubi sovrapposti che massimizzano l'ingresso della luce, accresce la flessibilità della casa e la rende adattabile a usi futuri.

Esta casa foi concebida como residência do próprio arquiteto, que teve especialmente em conta a sua sustentabilidade, tanto ecológica como económica. A simplicidade da estrutura, constituída por três cubos sobrepostos, que maximizam a entrada da luz, potencia a flexibilidade da casa e permite a sua adaptação a usos futuros.

Det här huset designades som bostad åt arkitekten själv, som tog fasta på att det skulle vara både ekologiskt och ekonomiskt hållbart. Enkelheten i konstruktionen, som utgörs av tre överlappande kuber som maximerar insläppet av ljus, ger huset flexibilitet så att det kan anpassas efter framtida användningsområden.

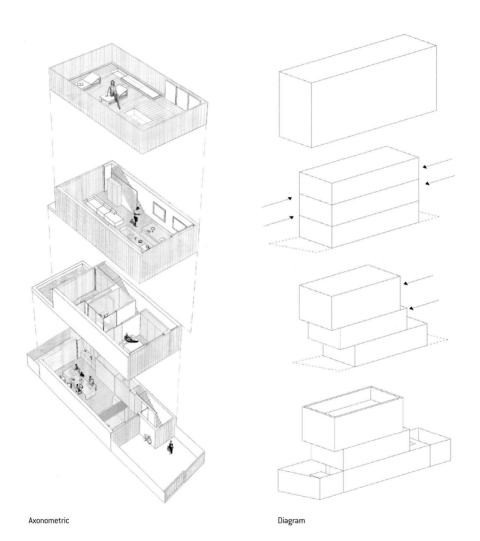

Axonometric   Diagram

For a sober dining room, use only a table, chairs, and a sideboard, and dispense with other elements.

Si vous cherchez à obtenir une salle à manger sobre, utilisez uniquement des meubles essentiels comme la table, les chaises et un buffet. Séparez-vous du reste.

Wenn Sie sich für ein nüchternes Esszimmer entscheiden, verwenden Sie lediglich Möbel wie Tisch, Stuhl und Anrichte und verzichten Sie auf andere Elemente.

Als je gaat voor een sobere inrichting van de eetkamer, beperk die dan tot een tafel, stoelen en misschien een dressoir en laat andere elementen achterwege.

Si te decantas por un comedor sobrio utiliza únicamente muebles como la mesa, las sillas y algún aparador, y prescinde de otros elementos.

Se propendi per una sala da pranzo sobria, utilizza solo mobili come la tavola, le sedie e qualche credenza, ed evita altri elementi.

Se pretender uma sala de jantar sóbria, utilize unicamente móveis como a mesa, cadeiras e eventualmente um aparador, dispensando quaisquer outros elementos.

Om du vill ha en dämpad matsalsinredning ska du ha enbart möbler som bord, stolar och skänk och välja bort andra saker.

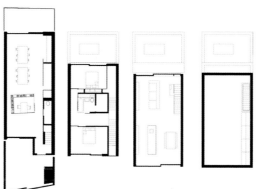

Floor plan

There are many ways to improve a home's energy efficiency. One is to place a skylight to allow the direct entry of light.

Il existe de nombreuses façons d'améliorer le rendement énergétique d'une maison. L'une d'entre elles consiste à installer une lucarne pour faire entrer la lumière directement.

Es gibt viele Formen, um die energetische Effizienz einer Wohnung zu steigern. Eine davon besteht in einem Oberlicht, das das Eindringen von direktem Licht ermöglicht.

Er zijn vele manieren om energie efficiënter te gebruiken in een woning, zoals het plaatsen van een dakraam waardoor het daglicht direct binnenvalt.

Hay muchas formas de mejorar la eficiencia energética de una vivienda. Una de ellas es la disposición de un lucernario que permita la entrada de luz directa.

Ci sono molti modi per migliorare l'efficienza energetica di una casa. Uno di questi è la collocazione di un lucernario che consenta l'ingresso di luce diretta.

Há muitas maneiras de melhorar a eficiência energética de uma casa. Uma delas é a disposição de uma claraboia que permita a entrada de luz direta.

Det finns många sätt att förbättra energieffektiviteten i hemmet. Ett är att skaffa ett takfönster som släpper in direkt ljus.

CHALET LA TRANSHUMANCE

NOÉ DUCHAUFOUR-LAWRENCE // Saint Martin de Belleville, France
© Vincent Leroux / © Thomas Mailaender: Johanna Grawunder during Wind Ceiling Light (Photo 2)

This family house in the French Alps is a far cry from the geometrical design of a traditional chalet. Inside, shapes emerge from the floor like small mountains that rise up over a valley. The result is fluid and modern: a set of lines and organic shapes that enhance the familial warmth.

Cette maison familiale située dans les Alpes françaises s'éloigne de la construction géométrique du chalet traditionnel. À l'intérieur, les formes surgissent du sol comme de petites montagnes fonctionnelles qui surplombent une vallée. Le résultat est fluide et moderne : un ensemble de lignes et de formes organiques qui alimentent la chaleur du foyer.

Dieses in den französischen Alpen gelegene Familienhaus distanziert sich von der geometrischen Konstruktion der traditionellen Chalets. In seinen Innenräumen treten die Formen aus dem Boden wie kleine funktionale Berge hervor, die sich aus dem Tal erheben. Das Ergebnis ist fließend und modern: ein Komplex aus organischen Linien und Formen, die zu der Wärme in der Familie beitragen.

Deze eengezinswoning in de Franse Alpen wijkt af van de traditionele vormgeving van de chaletstijl. De vloer van het interieur wordt gevormd door een functioneel reliëf van lage bergen rond een vallei. Het resultaat is vloeiend en modern: organische vormen en lijnen die de warme huiselijke sfeer versterken.

Esta casa familiar situada en los Alpes franceses se aleja de la construcción geométrica del chalé tradicional. En su interior, las formas emergen del suelo como pequeñas montañas funcionales que se alzan sobre un valle. El resultado es fluido y moderno: un conjunto de líneas y formas orgánicas que alimenta el calor familiar.

Questa casa familiare situata sulle Alpi francesi si allontana dalla costruzione geometrica dello chalet tradizionale. Al suo interno, le forme emergono dal pavimento come piccoli monticelli funzionali che si elevano su una valle. Il risultato è fluido e moderno: un insieme di linee e forme organiche che alimenta il calore familiare.

Esta residência familiar nos Alpes franceses afasta-se da construção geométrica do chalé tradicional. No interior, as vigas emergem do solo como pequenas montanhas funcionais que se elevam acima de um vale. O resultado é fluido e moderno: um conjunto de linhas e formas orgânicas que alimenta o aconchego em família.

Denna familjebostad i franska Alperna är geometriskt långt ifrån den traditionella bergsstugan. Invändigt stiger formerna från golvet som små funktionella berg som reser sig över en dal. Resultatet är jämnt och modernt: en uppsättning linjer och organiska former som ger en välbekant värme.

This design aims to generate an elevation that is modern, transparent, and minimalist, with lots of light.

Le design architectural cherchait à produire une volumétrie moderne, transparente et minimaliste, avec beaucoup de lumière.

Ziel des architektonischen Designs war eine moderne, transparente und minimalistische Volumetrie mit viel Licht.

Het gerealiseerde ontwerp heeft geleid tot een moderne, transparante en minimalistische ruimte met veel licht.

El diseño arquitectónico buscaba generar una volumetría moderna, transparente y minimalista, con mucha luz.

Il progetto architettonico puntava a generare una volumetria moderna, trasparente e minimalista, con molta luce.

O projeto arquitetónico tinha como objetivo criar uma volumetria moderna, transparente e minimalista, com muita luz.

Den arkitektoniska utformningen ville skapa en modern, öppen och minimalistisk volym, med massor av ljus.

The solidity of some materials, such as concrete, creates a feeling of firmness that blends perfectly with the visual purity of the spaces.

Le fait que certains matériaux tels que le ciment soient hermétiques crée une impression de fermeté qui se combine à la perfection avec les espaces épurés.

Die Geschlossenheit einiger Materialien wie Beton schafft ein Gefühl von Stabilität, die bis zur Perfektion mit der visuellen Reinheit der Räume kombiniert wird.

De dichtheid van sommige materialen zoals beton geeft een gevoel van stevigheid die zich perfect laat plaatsen tegenover de visuele zuiverheid van de ruimte.

La hermeticidad de algunos materiales como el hormigón crea una sensación de firmeza que combina a la perfección con la pureza visual de los espacios.

L'ermeticità di alcuni materiali come il cemento crea un senso di solidità che si combina perfettamente con la purezza visiva degli spazi.

A impenetrabilidade de certos materiais, como o betão, gera uma sensação de firmeza, que se combina na perfeição com a pureza visual dos espaços.

Tätheten hos vissa material, som betong, skapar en känsla av fasthet som passar perfekt i kombination med rummens visuella renhet.

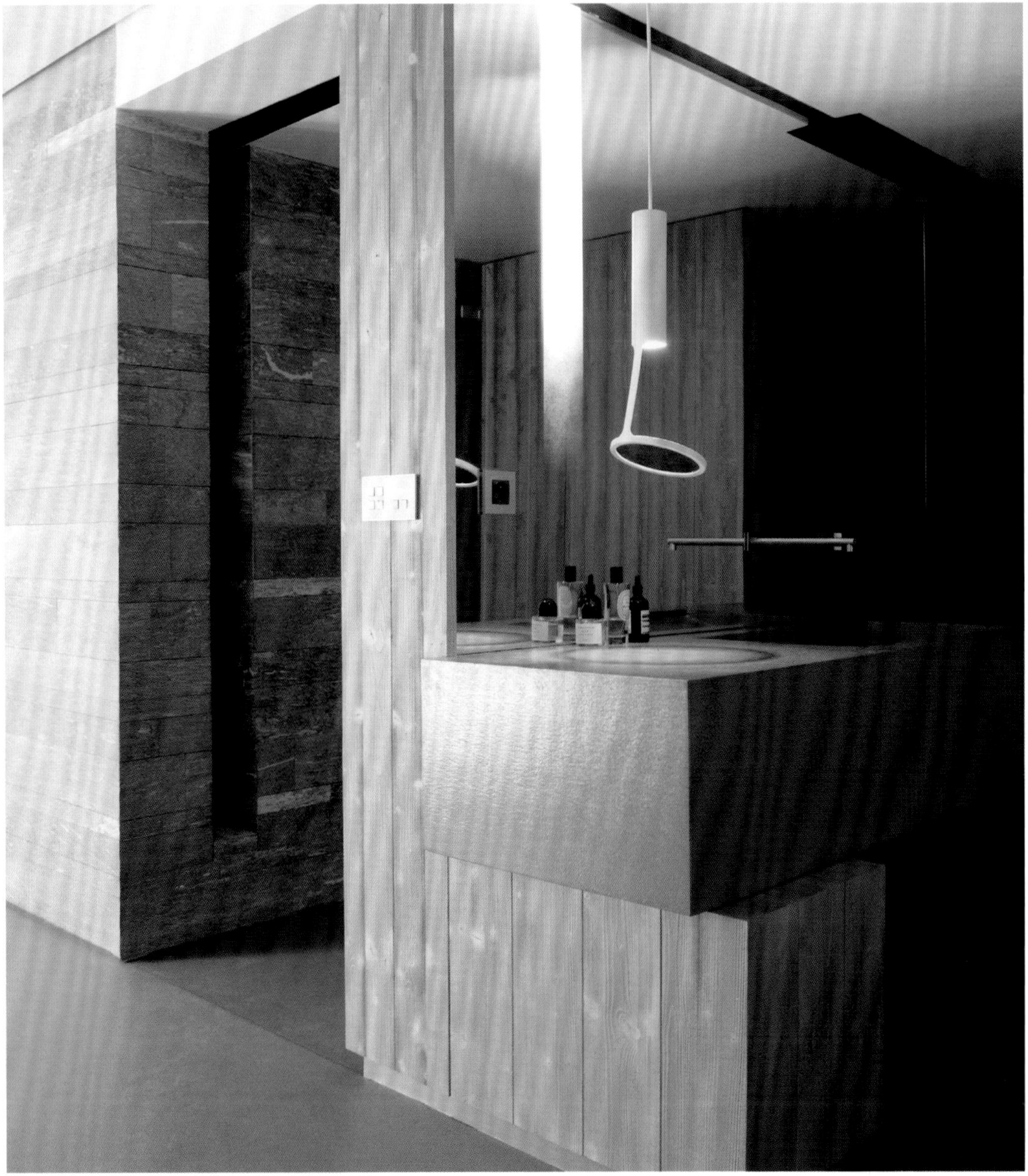

CHELSEA HILL HOUSE

KARIOUK ASSOCIATES // Chelsea, Canada
© Christian Lalonde / Photolux Studio

It was a challenge to convert this small house into a space that would include several areas without compartmentalizing them. Although the ground floor is mostly the teenagers' domain and the first floor the adults', both levels are connected by the two-storey entrance and the passageway underneath.

La transformation de cette petite maison en un espace regroupant l'ensemble des espaces nécessaires à ses habitants sans pour autant les compartimenter a été un vrai défi. Alors que le rez-de-chaussée est destiné aux adolescents et le premier étage aux adultes, les deux niveaux sont connectés sur la hauteur par un escalier et sur la longueur par une coursive.

Es war eine große Herausforderung, dieses kleine Haus in einen Ort zu verwandeln, der alle nötigen Räume für seine Bewohner beinhalten würde, ohne diese aber teilen zu müssen. Obwohl das Erdgeschoss eher für die Jugendlichen bestimmt war und das erste Obergeschoss für die Erwachsenen, sind beide Ebenen durch den Eingang, der sich über beide Etagen zieht, und den unteren Flur verbunden.

Het was een hele kluif om dit kleine huis om te vormen naar een ruimte die alle standaardfuncties vervult maar niet in kleine kamertjes is opgedeeld. De begane grond is het terrein van de jongeren en de eerste etage dat van de ouders. Beide lagen zijn met elkaar verbonden door een toegang naar beide delen en met een ondergelegen doorgang.

Era un reto convertir esta pequeña casa en un espacio que incluyera todas las áreas necesarias para sus habitantes, pero sin compartimentarlas. Aunque la planta baja está más dedicada a los adolescentes y el primer piso, a los adultos, ambos niveles están conectados por la entrada a dos alturas y el pasillo que hay debajo.

Trasformare questa piccola casa in uno spazio che includesse tutte le aree necessarie per i suoi abitanti, ma senza dividerle in compartimenti, rappresentava una sfida. Anche se il piano terra è prevalentemente dedicato agli adolescenti e il primo piano agli adulti, entrambi i livelli sono collegati dall'ingresso a due altezze e dal corridoio sottostante.

A transformação desta pequena casa num espaço que incluísse todas as áreas necessárias aos seus habitantes sem as compartimentar constituiu um verdadeiro desafio. Embora o andar de baixo esteja mais dedicado aos adolescentes e o de cima aos adultos, ambos estão ligados pela entrada de duplo pé-direito e pelo corredor que há por baixo.

Det var en utmaning att göra om det här lilla huset till något som omfattar allt som de boende behöver, utan att dela upp det. Trots att bottenvåningen är mer tillägnad ungdomarna och övervåningen tillhör de vuxna är båda våningarna sammanbundna genom entrén och hallen som ligger under den.

Dialogue is created by the transparent facade between the open communal areas.

Les espaces communs se prolongent à l'extérieur grâce à une façade transparente.

Die Gemeinschaftsbereiche verbinden sich durch die durchsichtige Fassade mit der offenen Gegenseite.

De gemeenschappelijke delen staan in contact met het open gedeelte via de transparante voorzijde.

Las áreas comunes dialogan con la contraparte abierta a través de la fachada transparente.

Le aree comuni dialogano con la controparte aperta tramite la facciata trasparente.

As áreas comuns dialogam com a parte aberta através de uma fachada transparente.

De gemensamma utrymmena öppnar en dialog mot den öppna naturen genom den transparenta fasaden.

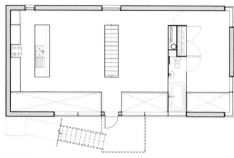

Floor plan

To define spaces, choose balanced and elegant compositions without breaking the visual relationship between them.

Optez pour des compositions équilibrées et élégantes au moment de définir les espaces, sans briser le lien visuel entre eux.

Wählen Sie ausgeglichene und elegante Kompositionen, wenn Sie die Räume definieren, ohne dabei mit ihrer visuellen Verbindung zu brechen.

Bedenk elegante en evenwichtige composities bij het definiëren van het interieur zonder dat de onderlinge visuele band wordt verbroken.

Opta por composiciones equilibradas y elegantes a la hora de definir los espacios, sin romper la relación visual entre ellos.

Opta per composizioni equilibrate ed eleganti al momento della definizione degli spazi, senza interrompere il rapporto visivo tra gli stessi.

Quando definir os espaços, opte por composições equilibradas e elegantes, sem romper a ligação visual entre eles.

Satsa på balanserade och eleganta kompositioner när du delar upp rummen, utan att bryta den visuella relationen mellan dem.

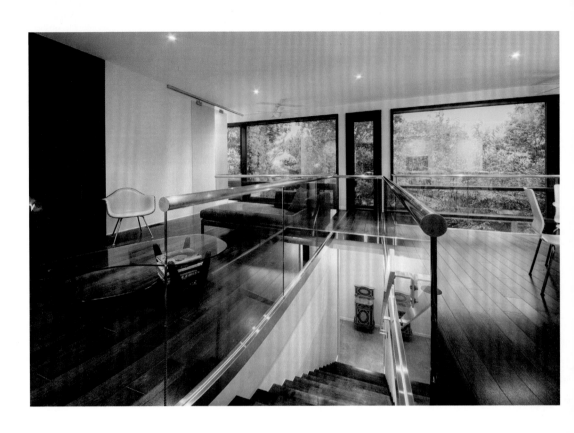

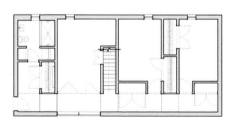

Floor plan

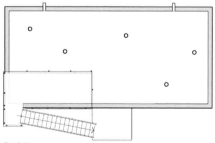

Roof plan

RESIDENCE TSAO

CHUN-TA TSAO / KC DESIGN STUDIO // Taipei, Taiwan
© Cola Chen

The key feature of this Taiwanese apartment is its revolving walls, which can instantly convert four rooms into an open floor plan. The floor is dark wood and the walls are white, which ensures that the furniture stands out and reflects the character of its owners.

L'élément clé de cet appartement taïwanais, ce sont les murs pivotants qui permettent de transformer en un rien de temps quatre chambres en un espace ouvert. Le sol est en bois sombre, les murs sont blancs, ce qui met à la fois en valeur le mobilier et reflète la personnalité des propriétaires.

Die Hauptelemente dieser Wohnung aus Taiwan sind die drehbaren Wände, die es ermöglichen, dass sich vier Zimmer kurzzeitig in einen Raum mit offenem Grundriss verwandeln. Der Boden ist aus dunklem Holz und die Wände sind weiß, wodurch die Möbel sich hervorheben und somit den Charakter ihrer Besitzer reflektieren.

De sleutelrol in dit appartement in Taiwan is weggelegd voor de roterende wanden die in een oogwenk vier kamers tot een grote open ruimte kunnen omvormen. De donkerhouten vloer en de witte wanden laten de meubels goed tot hun recht komen en deze geven iets prijs van het karakter van de eigenaren.

El elemento clave de este apartamento taiwanés son las paredes rotantes, que permiten que cuatro habitaciones se conviertan de forma instantánea en un espacio de planta abierta. El suelo es de madera oscura y las paredes, blancas, lo que consigue que los muebles destaquen y puedan reflejar el carácter de sus propietarios.

L'elemento chiave di questo appartamento taiwanese sono le pareti rotanti, che fanno in modo che quattro stanze si trasformino immediatamente in uno spazio a pianta aperta. Il pavimento è di legno scuro e le pareti bianche, tutto questo fa in modo che i mobili risaltino e possano riflettere il carattere dei loro proprietari.

O elemento essencial deste apartamento taiwanês são as paredes giratórias, que permitem que quatro divisões se transformem instantaneamente num espaço de planta aberta. O chão de madeira escura e as paredes brancas fazem com que os móveis sobressaiam e possam refletir a personalidade dos seus proprietários.

Den viktigaste delen av denna taiwanesiska lägenhet är de vändbara väggarna, som gör att fyra rum omedelbart kan förvandlas till öppen planlösning. Golvet är av mörkt trä och väggarna, som är vita, gör att möblerna framträder och kan återspegla ägarnas karaktär.

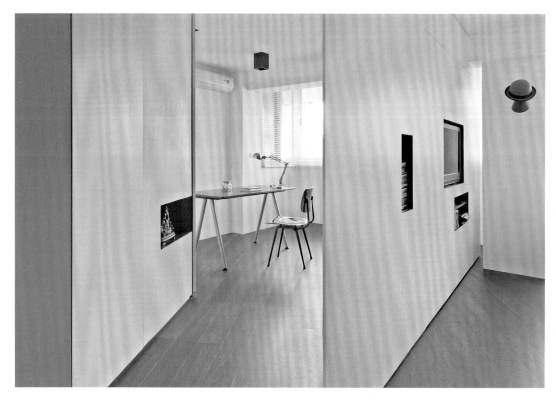

Try this idea to achieve intimacy: an aesthetically sober and multipurpose dividing screen.

Si vous envisagez de diviser l'espace pour obtenir plus d'intimité dans certaines pièces, inspirez-vous de cet écran de cloisonnement à l'esthétique sobre et multifonctionnelle.

Wenn Sie daran denken, den Raum zu teilen, um in einigen Bereichen für mehr Privatsphäre zu sorgen, verwenden Sie einen teilenden Bildschirm, ästhetisch nüchtern und multifunktional.

Voor meer intimiteit in een grote ruimte kun je deze onderverdelen in kleinere kamers met een wandscherm: esthetisch verantwoord, sober en multifunctioneel.

Si estás pensando en dividir el espacio para lograr intimidad en algunas estancias, considera esta idea de pantalla divisoria, estéticamente sobria y multifuncional.

Se stai pensando di suddividere lo spazio per acquisire intimità in alcune stanze, considera questa idea dello schermo divisorio, esteticamente sobrio e polivalente.

Se está a pensar em dividir o espaço para conseguir maior intimidade em algumas zonas, considere esta ideia de ecrã separador, esteticamente sóbria e multifuncional.

Om du funderar på att dela upp bostaden för få avskildhet i vissa rum, kan du titta på den här idén om en delningsskärm som är estetiskt dämpad och multifunktionell.

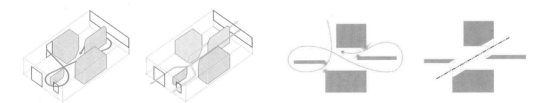

Diagram

Open spaces and airy arrangements with light furniture and pale colours convey a feeling of spaciousness and brightness in a home.

Pour qu'une maison donne une impression de grandeur et de luminosité, il faut privilégier les espaces ouverts et les agencements épurés avec un mobilier léger et des couleurs claires.

Damit in einer Wohnung das Gefühl von Größe und Helligkeit entsteht, muss man offene Räume und durchsichtige Raumteiler mit einem leichten Mobiliar und klaren Farben wählen.

Voor meer licht en ruimte in een woning: laat de ruimte open of plaats transparante scheidingen, plaats lichte meubels en gebruik zachte kleuren.

Para que una vivienda transmita una sensación de amplitud y luminosidad, hay que apostar por los espacios abiertos y las distribuciones diáfanas con un mobiliario liviano y colores claros.

Affinché una casa trasmetta un senso di grandezza e luminosità, bisogna scommettere sugli spazi aperti e le distribuzioni luminose con un arredamento leggero e colori chiari.

Para conseguir que a casa transmita uma sensação de amplitude e luminosidade, há que apostar nos espaços abertos e numa distribuição transparente, com mobiliário leve e de cores claras.

För att ett hem ska utstråla rymd och ljus måste man välja öppna ytor och luftiga fördelningar med lätta möbler och ljusa färger.

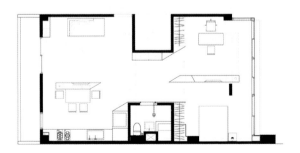

Floor plan

BEN AMI HOUSE

SHILO BENAROYA architecture office // Ramat Gan, Israel
© Friederike von Rauch

The family needed privacy, so a house was created using two boxes: one for public areas and another for private areas. This rational construction reflects the compact terrain and the desire for structural clarity in the house, which is made to appear wider using spatial continuity.

La famille désirait préserver son intimité. Il en résulte une maison composée de deux volumes : l'un pour les zones communes et l'autre pour les espaces privés. Il s'agit ici d'une construction rationnelle qui reflète un terrain étroit et le désir d'une structure claire, qui semble plus large grâce à la continuité des espaces.

Die Familie wollte Privatsphäre und daher wurde ein Haus aus zwei Teilen gebaut: Einer für die öffentlichen Räume und der andere für die privaten. Hierbei handelt es sich um eine rationale Konstruktion, die die Verdichtung des Bodens und den Wunsch nach Klarheit in der Struktur des Hauses reflektiert, das aufgrund seiner Kontinuität als sehr breit wahrgenommen wird.

Het gezin dat in dit huis woont, had behoefte aan privacy. Daarom zijn er twee blokken: een voor de gemeenschappelijke ruimtes en een voor de privéruimtes. De constructie is rationeel, het weerspiegelt de compacte afmetingen van het perceel en de wens om een duidelijke structuur aan te brengen die breed aandoet, doordat de ruimtes in elkaar overlopen.

La familia necesitaba privacidad, por eso se compuso una casa formada por dos cajas: una para las áreas públicas y otra para las privadas. Se trata de una construcción racional que refleja la compactación del terreno y el deseo de claridad en la estructura de la casa, que se percibe ancha debido a la continuidad de los espacios.

La famiglia aveva bisogno di privacy, per questo è stata realizzata una casa formata da due vani: uno per le aree pubbliche e un altro per quelle private. Si tratta di una costruzione razionale che rispecchia la compattezza del terreno e il desiderio di trasparenza nella struttura della casa, percepita larga grazie alla continuità degli spazi.

A família precisava de privacidade, pelo que se criou uma casa formada por duas caixas: uma para as áreas sociais e outra para as privadas. Trata-se de uma construção racional que reflete a compactação do terreno e o desejo de claridade na estrutura da casa, que parece ampla devido à continuidade dos espaços.

Familjen behövde avskildhet, så man skapade ett hus bestående av två sektioner: ett för gemensamma utrymmen och ett för privata. Det är en rationell konstruktion som återspeglar de komprimerade utrymmena och önskan om klarhet i husets struktur, som uppfattas som brett på grund av kontinuiteten mellan utrymmena.

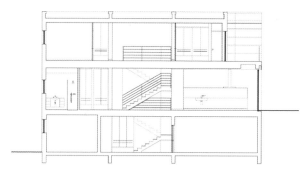

Section

Section

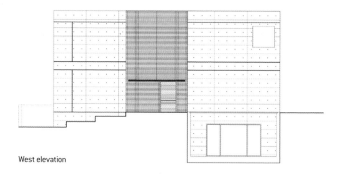

West elevation

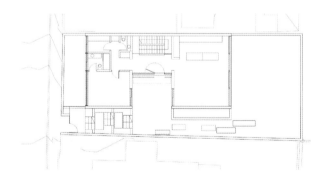

Ground floor

First floor

Kitchens have ceased to be closed places. Open to the outside, they assume new roles: a study area, a place to watch television, or a family gathering spot.

Les cuisines ont cessé d'être un lieu fermé pour s'ouvrir à l'extérieur en se dotant de nouvelles fonctions, comme se réunir en famille, étudier ou regarder la télévision.

Die Küche ist kein geschlossener Ort mehr und öffnet sich nach außen, indem sie neue Formen annimmt, wie zum Beispiel als Gemeinschaftsraum für die Familie oder als Fernsehzimmer.

De keuken is niet langer een afgesloten ruimte, maar opent zich naar buiten en leent zich voor nieuwe functies zoals tafelen met familie, studeren en televisiekijken.

Las cocinas han dejado de ser un lugar cerrado para abrirse al exterior asumiendo nuevas funciones, como reunirse en familia, estudiar o ver la televisión.

Le cucine smettono di essere un ambiente chiuso per aprirsi all'esterno acquisendo nuove funzioni, come quella di ritrovarsi in famiglia, studiare o vedere la televisione.

As cozinhas deixaram de ser um lugar fechado, abrindo-se para o exterior e sendo usadas para outros propósitos, como estar em família, estudar ou ver televisão.

Köken har gått från att vara slutna utrymmen till att öppna sig mot vardagsrummen och få nya roller, som en som samlingsplats för familjen där man kan läsa läxor och titta på TV.

HOUSE IN TAMATSU

KENJI IDO / IDO, KENJI ARCHITECTURAL STUDIO // Osaka, Japan
© Yohei Sasakura

This house in Osaka was designed for a family of four. The main requirement was that the family zone (dining room, living room, and kitchen) be wide, open, and filled with natural light. To achieve this, the second floor was rotated by 14 degrees. The stairs are especially impressive, appearing to float in space.

Cette maison située à Osaka a été conçue par une famille composée de quatre membres. Leur souhait principal, c'était que la partie familiale (la salle à manger, le salon et la cuisine) soit large, ouverte et lumineuse. Pour créer un tel espace, le volume du deuxième étage est à présent incliné à 14°. Les escaliers se démarquent particulièrement de l'ensemble et paraissent flotter dans le vide.

Dieses Haus liegt in Osaka und wurde für eine vierköpfige Familie gebaut. Die Hauptbedingung war, dass die familiären Räume (Esszimmer, Wohnzimmer und Küche) breit, offen und voller Sonnenlicht sind. Um dies zu ermöglichen, wurde das Volumen der Wohnung um 14° gedreht. Besonders treten die Treppen hervor, die den Anschein erwecken, als ob sie in einem leeren Raum schweben.

Dit huis in Osaka is ontworpen voor een gezin van vier. De voornaamste eis van de bewoners was een leefruimte (eetkamer, woonkamer en keuken) die breed en ruim is en waar het daglicht binnenvalt. Om die reden werd de tweede etage veertien graden gedraaid. Bijzonder zijn de traptreden die lijken te zweven in het luchtledige.

Esta casa situada en Osaka fue diseñada para una familia de cuatro miembros. El requisito principal era que la zona familiar (comedor, sala de estar y cocina) fuera ancha, abierta y tuviera luz natural. Para conseguirlo, el volumen del segundo piso se rotó 14°. Destacan especialmente las escaleras, que parecen flotar en el vacío.

Questa casa ubicata a Osaka è stata progettata per una famiglia di quattro componenti. Il requisito principale era che la zona familiare (sala da pranzo, salotto e cucina) fosse ampia, aperta e dotata di luce naturale. Per poterlo ottenere, il volume del secondo piano è stato ruotato di 14°. Si distinguono in particolare le scale, che sembrano fluttuare nel vuoto.

Esta casa situada em Osaka foi concebida para uma família de quatro elementos. O principal requisito era que a zona familiar (sala de jantar, sala de estar e cozinha) fosse ampla e aberta, e recebesse luz natural. Para isso, o volume do andar superior foi rodado 14°. Destacam-se especialmente as escadas, que parecem flutuar no vazio.

Detta hus som ligger i Osaka har designats för en familj på fyra. Det viktigaste kravet var att familjeutrymmena (matsal, vardagsrum och kök) skulle vara stora, öppna och ha dagsljus. För att uppnå detta har volymen med den andra våningen vridits 14°. Särskilt anmärkningsvärd är trappan som tycks flyta i ett vakuum.

Create the greatest possible sense of spaciousness, even if the space is small. Remove unnecessary corridors, doors, and walls.

Conférez une impression d'ampleur maximale à votre espace, même s'il n'est pas grand. Il est envisageable de supprimer des couloirs, des portes ou des cloisons inutiles.

Schaffen Sie so viel Größe wie nur möglich, obwohl der Raum sehr klein ist. Unnötige Gänge, Türen oder Trennwände werden abgeschafft.

Creëer zo veel mogelijk een gevoel van ruimte, ook al is de ruimte beperkt. Sloop overbodige gangen, deuren en tussenwanden.

Crea la mayor sensación de amplitud posible, aunque el espacio no sea grande. Puedes eliminar pasillos, puertas o tabiques innecesarios.

Offri il maggior senso di grandezza possibile, anche se lo spazio non è grande. Possono essere eliminati corridoi, porte o tramezzi superflui.

Proporcione a maior sensação de amplitude possível, mesmo que o espaço não seja grande. Podem eliminar-se corredores, portas e divisórias que não sejam necessários.

Försök få till största möjliga känsla av rymd, även om utrymmet inte är så stort. Man kan ta bort hallar, dörrar och väggar som inte behövs.

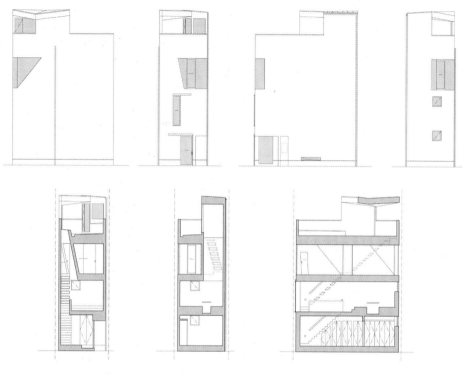

Elevations and sections

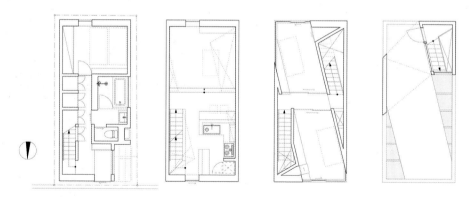

Plans

Natural light has always been a scarce commodity inside houses. These days, houses are designed to capture it and enhance it to the fullest.

La lumière naturelle a toujours été un bien rare à l'intérieur des maisons. Dans les habitats d'aujourd'hui, tout est fait pour capter et exploiter la lumière au maximum.

Das natürliche Tageslicht ist im Inneren der Häuser sehr knapp gewesen. Jetzt wird alles nur Mögliche versucht, um das Licht einzufangen und es zu maximieren.

Daglicht is altijd een schaars goed geweest in het interieur. Tegenwoordig streven ontwerpers ernaar om zo veel mogelijk het licht op te vangen en het goed te benutten.

La luz natural siempre ha sido un bien escaso en el interior de las casas. Ahora las viviendas hacen lo posible por captarla y potenciarla al máximo.

La luce naturale è sempre stata un bene poco presente all'interno delle case. Ora le abitazioni fanno il possibile per catturarla e potenziarla al massimo.

A luz natural foi desde sempre um bem escasso no interior das casas. Atualmente, faz-se o possível por captá-la e potenciar ao máximo.

Dagsljus har alltid varit en bristvara i våra hem. Idag har bostäderna möjlighet att fånga upp det och utnyttja det till max.

PENTHOUSE BERLIN

OSKAR FABIAN GBR ARCHITECTURE // Berlin, Germany
© Gerrit Engel

Remodelling this Berlin apartment's attic required the creation of a single space. Installing a mirror made of unequal pieces, divided and positioned one by one, lent a dynamic and capricious air to the space, animating it by fragmenting its surface.

Pour réaménager les combles d'un appartement berlinois, il a fallu créer un espace unitaire. Pour ce faire, il a finalement été décidé d'installer un miroir. Formé de pièces inégales, divisées et disposées une à une, il apporte une touche dynamique et capricieuse à la pièce, et l'égaye avec sa surface fragmentée.

Für die Umstrukturierung dieses Penthouses in ein Appartement in Berlin war es nötig, einen einheitlichen Raum zu schaffen. Letztendlich entschied man sich für den Einbau eines Spiegels. Dieser Spiegel aus ungleich zerteilten Stücken, die einzeln angeordnet sind, verleiht dem Raum ein dynamisches und verspieltes Gefühl und belebt ihn durch seine zerstückelte Oberfläche.

De eenheid in stijl bij deze make-over van een penthouse in Berlijn werd gecreëerd door het plaatsen van spiegelglas dat in ongelijke stukken over de ruimte is verdeeld. Deze versplintering van de oppervlakte zorgt voor een dynamische en eigenzinnige sfeer.

Para la remodelación de este ático de un apartamento de Berlín era necesario crear un espacio unitario, y finalmente se optó por la instalación de un espejo. Este, formado por piezas desiguales divididas y colocadas una a una, aporta un aire dinámico y caprichoso a la estancia, animándola mediante la fragmentación de su superficie.

Per la ristrutturazione di questo attico di un appartamento di Berlino era necessario creare uno spazio unitario, e alla fine si è optato per l'installazione di uno specchio. Questo, formato da parti diverse, divise e collocate una a una, conferisce un'aria dinamica e bizzarra alla stanza, vivacizzandola grazie alla frammentazione della sua superficie.

Para a remodelação deste sótão de um apartamento em Berlim era necessário criar um espaço unitário, acabando por se optar pela instalação de um espelho. Este, formado por peças desiguais separadas e colocadas uma a uma, confere um ar dinâmico e fantasioso à sala, animando-a através da fragmentação da sua superfície.

För renoveringen denna av takvåning i Berlin var det nödvändigt att skapa en gemensam plats, och slutligen valde man att installera en spegel. Den består av ojämna bitar som har hängts upp tätt ihop, vilket ger en dynamisk och nyckfull känsla åt rummet, och livar upp genom ytans fragmentering.

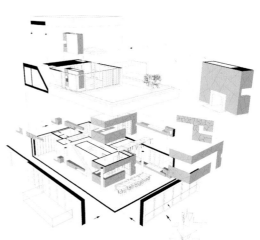

Exploded axonometric

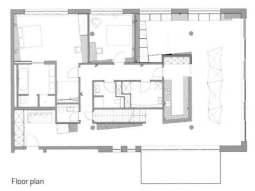

Floor plan

199

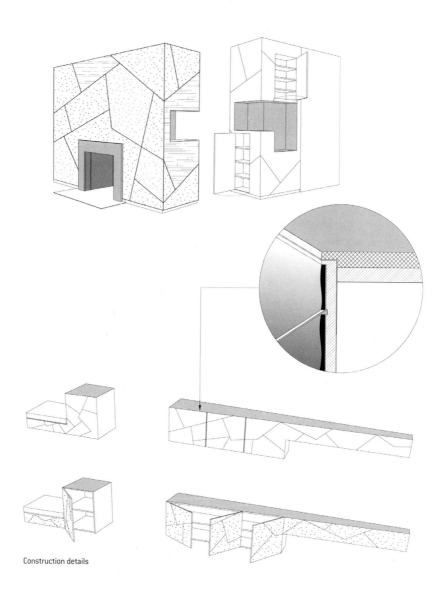

Construction details

In this area of the house, communal spaces like the kitchen, dining room, and lounge coexist harmoniously. The materials lend homogeneity and lightness.

Dans cet espace se combinent harmonieusement différentes parties communes, comme la cuisine, la salle à manger et le salon. L'homogénéité et la légèreté sont obtenues grâce aux matériaux choisis.

Hier fließen auf harmonische Weise verschiedene Gemeinschaftsräume zusammen, wie Küche, Ess- und Wohnzimmer. Die Homogenität und Leichtigkeit wird mit den ausgewählten Materialien erreicht.

De gemeenschappelijke delen, zoals de keuken, de eetkamer en de salon, delen harmonieus dezelfde ruimte. De homogeniteit en de lichtheid worden verkregen door de gekozen materialen.

En esta área conviven armoniosamente diferentes espacios comunes, como la cocina, el comedor y el salón. La homogeneidad y la ligereza se consiguen con los materiales escogidos.

In quest'area convivono in armonia vari spazi comuni, come la cucina, la sala da pranzo e il salone. L'omogeneità e la leggerezza si raggiungono con i materiali scelti.

Nesta área convivem em harmonia diferentes espaços comuns, como a cozinha, a sala de jantar e a sala. A homogeneidade e leveza conseguem-se com materiais selecionados.

I det här utrymmet samverkar husets olika gemensamma utrymmen på ett harmoniskt sätt, som kök, matsal och vardagsrum. Homogeniteten och den lättheten uppnås med väl valda material.

MAFF APARTMENT

QUEESTE ARCHITECTEN // The Hague, Netherlands
© Teun van den Dries

This 30-square-metre (323-square-feet) hotel room, in the attic of a private house in The Hague, needed to incorporate multiple functions in a very limited space, which also had to be unique and luxurious. Amid the smoothness created by rounded shapes and white surfaces, the striking orange of the sofa alludes to the roofs of The Hague.

Cette chambre d'hôtes de 30 m², située dans le grenier d'une maison privée à La Haye, devait comporter de multiples fonctions dans un espace très limité, en plus d'être unique et luxueuse. La douceur créée par les formes arrondies et les surfaces blanches fait ressortir le canapé orange qui évoque les toits de La Haye.

Dieses Hotelzimmer ist 30m² groß und liegt in einem Penthouse in einem Privathaus in Den Haag. Es musste auf sehr kleinem Raum zahlreiche Funktionen erfüllen und erscheint außerdem einzigartig und luxuriös. In der Sanftheit, die die runden Formen und weißen Oberflächen geschaffen haben, sticht das Orange des Sofas hervor, das an die Dächer in Den Haag erinnert.

Binnen de beperkte ruimte van deze gastenkamer van 30 m² op de zolderverdieping van een privéhuis in Den Haag komen verschillende functies samen. Niettemin is de ruimte uniek en luxueus. In de zachte sfeer, gecreëerd door de ronde vormen en de witte vlakken, springt de oranje bank, die zinspeelt op de Haagse daken, in het oog.

Esta habitación de hotel de 30 m², situada en el ático de una casa privada de La Haya, tenía que incorporar múltiples funciones en un espacio muy limitado, además de resultar única y lujosa. En la suavidad creada por las formas redondeadas y las superficies blancas, sobresale el naranja del sofá, que alude a los tejados de La Haya.

Questa camera di hotel di 30 m², situata nell'attico di una casa privata dell'Aia, doveva comprendere molteplici funzioni in uno spazio molto limitato, oltre a risultare unica e lussuosa. Tra la morbidezza creata dalle forme arrotondate e dalle superfici bianche, si distingue l'arancione del divano, che richiama i tetti dell'Aia.

Pretendia-se que este quarto de aluguer de 30 m², situado no sótão de uma casa privada em Haia, para além de original e luxuoso, incluísse múltiplas funcionalidades num espaço muito limitado. Em contraste com a suavidade criada pelas formas arredondadas e as superfícies brancas, sobressai o cor de laranja do sofá, que evoca os telhados de Haia.

Detta hotellrum på 30 m², som ligger på vinden till ett privat hus i Haag, måste införliva flera funktioner i ett mycket begränsat utrymme, samt vara unikt och lyxigt. En mjukhet som skapas av rundade former och vita ytor framträder genom den orange soffan, som anspelar på Haags hustak.

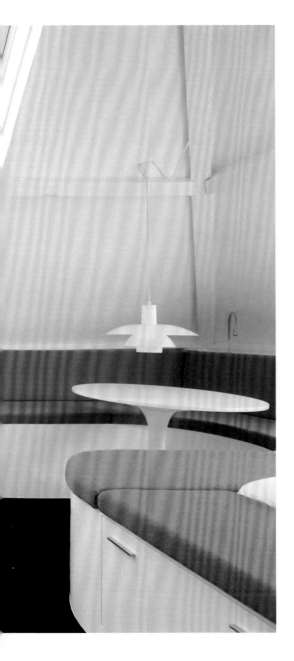

Section

Section

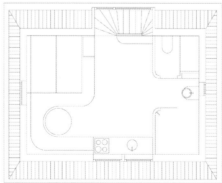

Floor plan

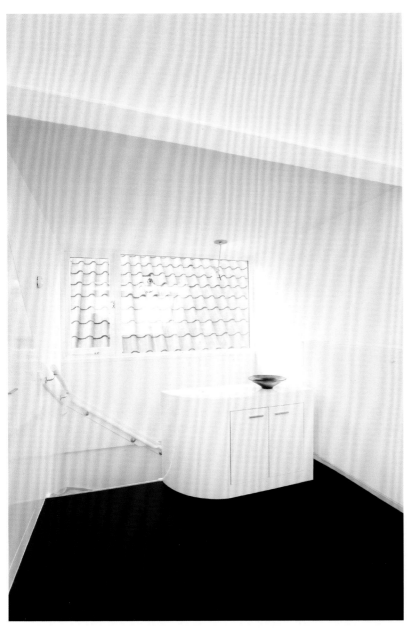

Create continuous spaces to make the most of direct light from outside.

Créez des espaces continus. Cela vous permettra de bénéficier d'une lumière directe en provenance de l'extérieur.

Schaffen Sie einen durchgängigen Raum. Sie werden merken, dass sie vom direkten Sonnenlicht profitieren.

Creëer doorlopende ruimtes. Zo zorg je ervoor dat in alle ruimtes voldoende direct licht binnenvalt.

Crea espacios continuos. Conseguirás que se beneficien de la luz directa que proviene del exterior.

Crea spazi continui. Farai in modo che possano beneficiare della luce diretta che viene dall'esterno.

Crie espaços contínuos. Consegue, desse modo, que recebam a luz direta que vem do exterior.

Skapa oavbrutna utrymmen. Du kommer att få ljuset utifrån att nå in överallt.

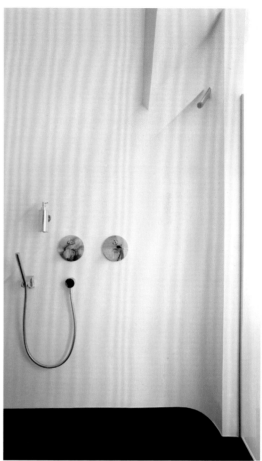

BARKER RESIDENCE

davidclovers // Hong Kong, China
© Almond Chu

The renovation of this apartment with dazzling views over Hong Kong's Victoria Harbour focused on enhancing the most powerful aspects of the existing design. The staircase that winds between the two floors is even more exceptional than the subtly sloping walls that group various functions together.

Avec des vues des plus impressionnantes sur le port de Victoria à Hong Kong, la rénovation de cet appartement a consisté essentiellement à localiser les éléments les plus forts du design existant pour les mettre en valeur. Bien plus que les murs subtilement inclinés aux fonctions variées, l'escalier qui serpente entre les deux niveaux est tout particulièrement frappant.

Mit einigen überwältigenden Ausblicken auf den Victoria Hafen von Hong Kong legte man bei der Renovierung dieser Wohnung Wert darauf, die wichtigsten Punkte des bestehenden Designs zu finden, um diese hervorzuheben. Noch viel mehr als die leicht geneigten Wände, die diverse Funktionen vereinen, sticht die Treppe hervor, die sich durch die zwei Etagen schlängelt.

Dit appartement heeft een adembenemend uitzicht over de Victoria haven in Hong Kong. De renovatie was erop gericht om de sterke punten van het oorspronkelijke ontwerp nog beter te doen uitkomen. Zo hellen de muren, die meerdere functies vervullen, subtiel over, maar het is vooral de wenteltrap naar de tweede etage die nadrukkelijk aanwezig is.

Con unas deslumbrantes vistas sobre el puerto de Victoria de Hong Kong, la renovación de este apartamento se centró en localizar los puntos más potentes del diseño existente para realzarlos. Aún más que las paredes sutilmente inclinadas que aúnan diversas funciones, destaca la escalera que serpentea entre los dos pisos.

Con una vista sensazionale sul porto di Victoria di Hong Kong, la ristrutturazione di questo appartamento si è concentrata sull'individuazione dei punti dominanti del disegno esistente per enfatizzarli. Ancor di più delle pareti leggermente inclinate che racchiudono diverse funzioni, spicca la scala che serpenteggia tra i due piani.

A remodelação deste apartamento com deslumbrantes vistas sobre o porto de Victoria, em Hong Kong, centrou-se na identificação e realce dos pontos mais fortes do conjunto já existente. Mais ainda que as paredes ligeiramente inclinadas, cumprindo diversas funções, destaca-se a escada, que serpenteia entre os dois andares.

På grund av den bländande utsikten över Victoria-hamnen i Hong Kong kom renoveringen av lägenheten att fokusera på att hitta de bästa designpunkterna för att förbättra den. Ännu mer än de subtilt sluttande väggarna, som kombinerar flera funktioner, framträder trappan som slingrar sig mellan de två våningarna.

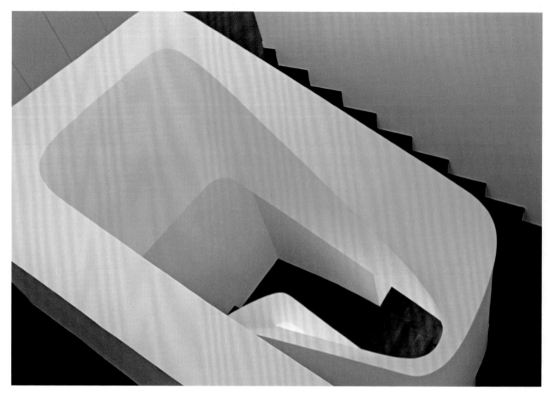

A stairway can bring movement to an area characterised by straight lines.

Le tracé des escaliers peut apporter du mouvement à une zone qui se caractérise par des lignes droites.

Der Entwurf der Treppen kann einem Raum mit geraden Linien ein Gefühl von Dynamik geben.

De vloeiende lijn van een trap kan beweging suggereren in een ruimte met verder alleen rechte lijnen.

El trazado de las escaleras puede transmitir movimiento a una zona caracterizada por las líneas rectas.

Il percorso delle scale può trasmettere movimento a una zona caratterizzata da linee rette.

O traçado das escadas pode conferir movimento a uma zona caracterizada pelas linhas retas.

Formen på trappan kan ge en känsla av rörelse till ett rum som annars kännetecknas av räta linjer.

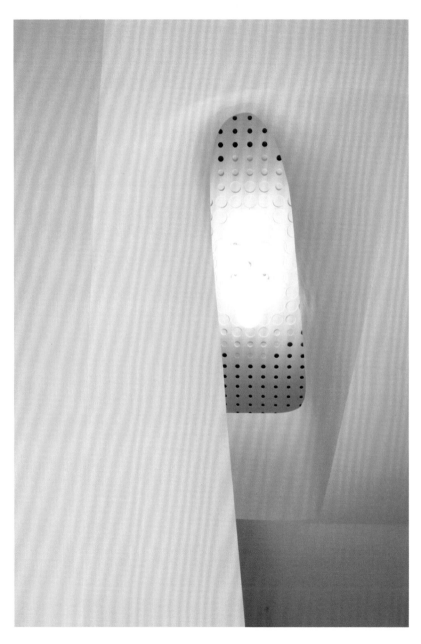

The shape of the staircase marks the smooth rhythm of different levels in the home.

La géométrie de l'escalier appose un rythme fluide aux différents niveaux de la maison.

Die Geometrie der Treppe kennzeichnet den fließenden Rhythmus der verschiedenen Ebenen in der Wohnung.

De vormgeving van de trap geeft het vloeiende ritme aan voor alle lagen in de woning.

La geometría de la escalera marca el ritmo fluido de los diferentes niveles de la vivienda.

La geometria della scala segna il ritmo fluido dei vari livelli della casa.

A geometria da escada marca o ritmo fluido dos diferentes níveis da casa.

Trappans geometri ger en flytande rytm mellan de olika våningsplanen i bostaden.

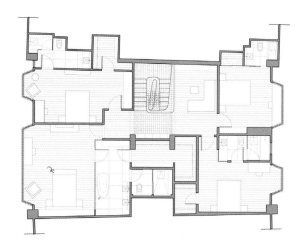

Second floor

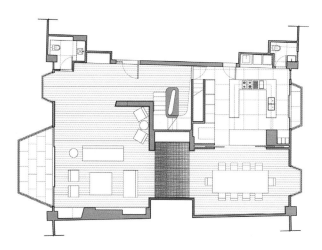

First floor

ROUNDED LOFT

LENKA KŘEMENOVÁ, DAVID MAŠTÁLKA / A1ARCHITECTS // Prague, Czech Republic
© David Maštálka / A1Architects

This project involved the conversion of an attic in a 1930s house in Prague. Some corners were rounded off to bring fluidity to the space. Two features stand out: the stainless steel net used as a bannister, and the bookshelves on the staircase, which look like a brick wall.

Cette maison située à Prague est le résultat de la rénovation d'un vieux grenier des années 1930. Pour que l'espace soit fluide, il a été décidé d'arrondir quelques angles. Deux éléments se détachent de l'ensemble : la rampe de l'escalier, un filet en acier inoxydable, et la bibliothèque près de l'escalier qui s'apparente à un mur de briques.

Dieses Haus in Prag entstand aus einer Umstrukturierung eines alten Penthouses der 30er Jahre. Damit der Raum fließend ist, wurden einige Kanten abgerundet. Zwei Elemente treten aus den übrigen hervor: Das Treppengeländer, ein Netz aus rostfreiem Stahl, und das Bücherregal in einer Treppennische, das einer Ziegelmauer ähnelt.

Deze woning in Praag was vroeger de zolderverdieping van een jaren dertig huis. Om de vormgeving vloeiender te maken, zijn sommige hoeken afgerond. De twee elementen die het meest in het oog springen, zijn de trapleuning met vlechtwerk van roestvrij staal en de bibliotheek onder de trap die van een afstand op een bakstenen muur lijkt.

Esta casa situada en Praga es la reconversión de un viejo ático de los años treinta. Para que el espacio fuera fluido, se decidió redondear algunas de las esquinas. Dos elementos sobresalen del resto: el pasamanos de la escalera, que es una red de acero inoxidable, y la librería en el hueco de la escalera, que parece un muro de ladrillos.

Questa casa situata a Praga è la conversione di un vecchio attico degli anni trenta. Per fare in modo che lo spazio fosse fluido, si è deciso di arrotondare alcuni degli angoli. Due elementi spiccano sul resto: il parapetto della scala, una rete di acciaio inox, e la libreria nel vano della scala, che ricorda un muro di mattoni.

Esta casa situada em Praga resulta da reconversão de um velho sótão dos anos 30. Para tornar o espaço fluido, decidiu-se arredondar algumas das esquinas. Dois elementos sobressaem do conjunto: o corrimão da escada, uma rede de aço inoxidável, e a estante no vão da escada, que parece um muro de tijolo.

Detta hus i Prag är en omvandling av en gammal vind från 30-talet. För att utrymmet ska få ett flöde valde man att runda av några av hörnen. Två saker sticker ut från resten: trappans räcke, ett nät av rostfritt stål, och bokhyllan i trappan, som ser ut som en tegelvägg.

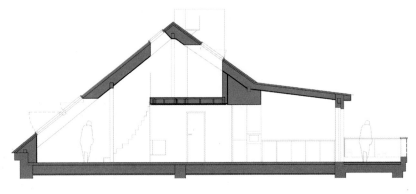

Section

Floor plan

Every staircase needs a bannister, regardless of its structure. In this case a simple net was chosen.

Tout escalier doit posséder une rampe, quelles que soient ses caractéristiques structurelles. Ici, un simple filet fait l'affaire.

Jede Treppe sollte ein Geländer besitzen, unabhängig von ihren strukturellen Merkmalen. In diesem Fall wurde ein einfaches Rot gewählt.

Elke trap heeft hoe dan ook een leuning, ongeacht de vormgeving. Hier werd gekozen voor een eenvoudig vlechtwerk.

Cualquier escalera debe tener su pasamanos, sin importar sus condiciones estructurales. En este caso se optó por una simple red.

Ogni scala deve avere il suo parapetto, indipendentemente dalle sue condizioni strutturali. In questo caso si è scelta una semplice rete.

Qualquer escada, sejam quais forem as suas características estruturais, deve ter o seu corrimão. Neste caso, optou-se por uma simples rede.

Alla trappor måste ha ledstång, oavsett strukturella förhållanden. I det här fallet valde man ett enkelt nät.

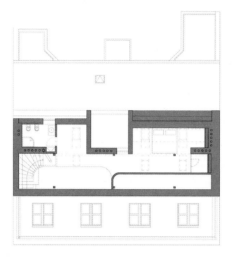

Floor plan

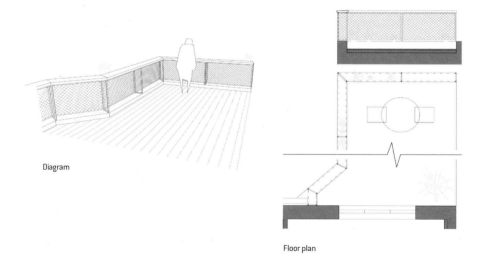

Diagram

Floor plan

AXIAL SYMPHONY

DESIGN SYSTEMS // Shenzhen, China
© Courtesy of Design Systems

The design of this apartment in the Chinese city of Shenzhen began with the idea that a symmetrical space fosters personal equilibrium. Thus the furniture in each functional space is arranged around a central axis so that the inhabitant is always at the centre of each zone, underlining his or her individuality.

Le design de cet appartement de la ville chinoise de Shenzhen part de l'idée que la création d'un espace symétrique favorise l'équilibre personnel. Ici, dans chaque espace fonctionnel, les meubles s'agencent par rapport à un axe central : ainsi, l'habitant se trouve toujours au centre de chaque zone, ce qui souligne son individualité.

Das Design dieses Appartements in der chinesischen Stadt Shenzhen teilt die Idee von einem symmetrischen Raum, der das persönliche Gleichgewicht hervorhebt. Daher befinden sich die Möbel an allen zweckmäßigen Orten um eine Zentralachse gelegen: Somit bleibt der Bewohner in jedem Raum im Mittelpunkt, was seine Individualität in den Vordergrund rückt.

Het ontwerp voor dit appartement in de Chinese stad Shenzhen stoelt op de idee dat symmetrie in het interieur goed is voor het persoonlijk evenwicht. Om die reden staan in elke functionele ruimte de meubels opgesteld rond een centraal punt. Zo bevindt de bewoner zich steeds in het centrum van de ruimte en bevestigt daarmee de eigen individualiteit.

El diseño de este apartamento en la ciudad china de Shenzhen parte de la idea de que la creación de un espacio simétrico favorece el equilibrio personal. Por ello, en cada espacio funcional los muebles se sitúan en torno a un eje central: así, el habitante siempre queda en el centro de cada zona, lo que subraya su individualidad.

Il progetto di questo appartamento nella cittadina cinese di Shenzhen parte dall'idea che la creazione di uno spazio simmetrico favorisce l'equilibrio personale. Per questo, in ciascuno degli spazi funzionali, i mobili sono collocati attorno a un asse centrale: così l'abitante rimane sempre al centro di ogni zona, sottolineandone l'individualità.

O projeto deste apartamento na cidade chinesa de Shenzhen parte da ideia de que a criação de um espaço simétrico favorece o equilíbrio pessoal. Por isso, em cada um dos espaços funcionais, os móveis situam-se em volta de um eixo central. Desta forma, o habitante fica sempre no centro de cada zona, o que reforça a sua individualidade.

Utformningen av denna lägenhet i den kinesiska staden Shenzhen kommer från tanken att skapandet av ett symmetriskt utrymme främjar personlig balans. Därför står möblerna i varje funktionellt utrymme runt en central axel: på det sättet är den boende alltid i mitten av varje zon, vilket understryker deras individualitet.

To lend dynamism to a Zen garden, create sculptural groups of sinuous forms, such as these small mounds.

Pour apporter une touche de dynamisme à un jardin zen, créez des groupes sculpturaux aux formes sinueuses comme ces petits monticules.

Um einem Zen-Garten etwas Dynamik zu verleihen, sollten Sie geschwungene Skulpturen, wie diese kleinen Hügel, verwenden.

Om een zentuin meer dynamiek te geven, kun je sculpturen met golvende lijnen plaatsen, zoals dit kleine berglandschap.

Para dotar de dinamismo a un jardín zen, crea grupos escultóricos de formas sinuosas, como estos pequeños montículos.

Per conferire dinamismo a un giardino zen, crea gruppi scultorei dalle forme sinuose, come questi piccoli monticelli.

Para conferir dinamismo a um jardim zen, crie grupos escultóricos de formas sinuosas, como estas pequenas elevações.

För att ge trädgården en dynamik av zen kan man skapa slingrande skulpturala grupper, som dessa små högar.

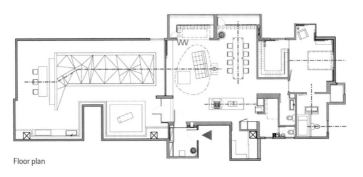

Floor plan

HOUSE MJ

KOMBINAT // Novo Mesto, Slovenia
© Matjaž Tančič, Klemen Ilovar

In a meadow on the edge of a forest and with views of the Slovenian city of Novo Mesto, this house has no hallways: the rooms are all accessed from the living room. Although the garage is separate from the house, its mottled surface establishes a connection between the two spaces.

Située dans un pré entre des maisons résidentielles et l'orée d'un bois, avec des vues sur la ville de Novo Mesto, en Slovénie, cette maison ne comporte aucun couloir : l'accès aux chambres se fait par le salon. Bien que le garage soit séparé de la maison, sa surface veinée établit une connexion entre les deux espaces.

Dieses Haus, das auf einer großen Wiese inmitten von Wohnhäusern und am Rande eines Waldes liegt und den Ausblick auf die slowenische Stadt Novo Mesto gewährt, besitzt keine Flure: In die jeweiligen Zimmer gelangt man über das Wohnzimmer. Obwohl sich die Garage nicht im Haus befindet, schafft seine gemaserte Oberfläche eine Verbindung zwischen beiden Räume.

Dit huis in Slovenië is gelegen in een weiland aan de rand van een bos tussen andere woningen en met uitzicht op de stad Novo Mesto. Het huis heeft geen gangen, vanuit de woonkamer kun je de andere kamers binnenlopen. Hoewel de garage losstaat van het huis, is ze met het huis verbonden door dezelfde bedekking van gevlamd hout.

Situada en una pradera entre casas residenciales y los márgenes de un bosque, con vistas a la ciudad de Novo Mesto, en Eslovenia, esta casa no tiene pasillos: se accede a las habitaciones desde la sala de estar. Aunque el garaje se encuentra separado de la casa, su superficie veteada establece una conexión entre ambos espacios.

Situata in un grande prato tra case residenziali ai margini di un bosco, con vista sulla città di Novo Mesto, in Slovenia, questa casa non è dotata di corridoi: si accede alle camere dal salotto. Nonostante il garage sia separato dalla casa, la sua superficie venata stabilisce un collegamento tra i due spazi.

Situada num prado, entre edifícios residenciais e a orla de uma floresta, com vista para a cidade de Novo Mesto, na Eslovénia, esta casa não tem corredores: o acesso aos quartos faz-se a partir da sala de estar. Embora a garagem se encontre separada da casa, a sua superfície com veios estabelece a ligação entre ambos os espaços.

På en äng mellan bostadsområdena, vid kanten av en skog och med utsikt över staden Novo Mesto i Slovenien, ligger detta hus som saknar hallar: rummen nås från vardagsrummet. Trots att garaget är fristående från huset ger de strimmiga ytorna ett samband mellan dem.

If you want a spacious lounge with minimal furniture, choose built-in shelves that will become a focal point.

Si vous désirez obtenir un salon spacieux avec peu de meubles, optez pour des étagères murales en guise de bibliothèque : elles se détacheront dans l'espace.

Wenn Sie auf der Suche nach einem weiten, mit wenigen Möbeln bestückten Raum sind, wählen Sie ummauerte Regale, die als Bibliothek dienen und sich in den zentralen Punkt verwandeln.

Als je een ruime salon wilt met weinig meubels kies dan voor wandelementen die dienst doen als bibliotheek en die het centrale aandachtspunt vormen.

Si buscas un salón espacioso y con pocos muebles opta por estantes amurados que sirvan de biblioteca y se conviertan en el punto focal.

Se sei alla ricerca di un salotto spazioso e con pochi mobili, opta per scaffali a muro che fungano da biblioteca e che diventino il punto focale.

Se pretende uma sala espaçosa e com poucos móveis, opte por prateleiras de parede, que sirvam de estante e se tornem o foco de atenção.

Om du söker en rymlig och glest inredd salong kan du välja inmurade hyllor som fungerar som bokhyllor och blir en blickpunkt.

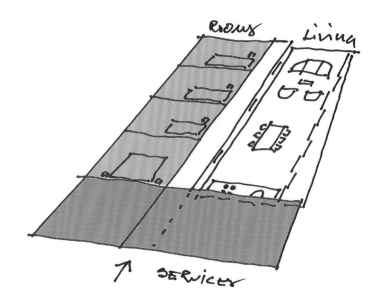

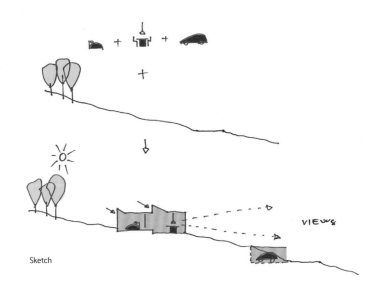

Sketch

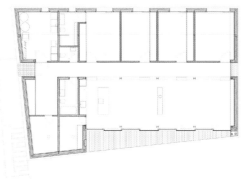

Floor plan

HOUSSEIN APARTMENT

TRIPTYQUE // São Paulo, Brazil
© Courtesy of Triptyque

This 300-square-metre apartment in São Paulo embraces holistic design: it is a completely artistic project, seeking to surprise with the creation of unexpected or unjustified spaces. Inside the house, the outstanding minimalist features include concrete, wood, stainless steel, and white walls.

Cet appartement de 300 m² à São Paulo embrasse le concept de design total : c'est un projet totalement artistique qui cherche à surprendre en créant des espaces inattendus ou gratuits. À l'intérieur de la maison, les éléments de style minimaliste ressortent tout particulièrement : le béton, le bois, l'acier inoxydable, les murs blancs...

Dieses 300m² große Appartement in São Paulo vertritt die Idee eines globalen Designs: Es ist ein rein künstlerisches Projekt, das durch die Schaffung von unerwarteten und ungerechtfertige Räumen verwundern will. Im Inneren des Hauses stechen Elemente in minimalistischem Stil hervor: Beton, Holz, rostfreier Stahl, weiße Wände...

Dit appartement van 300 m² in São Paulo omarmt het concept van totaaldesign. Het is een volledig artistiek project dat wil verrassen met onverwachte en ongerechtvaardige ruimtes. In het interieur vallen de minimalistische elementen op: beton, hout, roestvrij staal en witte muren.

Este apartamento de 300 m² en São Paulo abraza la idea de diseño global: es un proyecto enteramente artístico que busca la sorpresa mediante la creación de espacios inesperados o gratuitos. En el interior de la casa, destacan los elementos de estilo minimalista: hormigón, madera, acero inoxidable, paredes blancas...

Questo appartamento di 300 m² a San Paolo adotta l'idea di design globale: si tratta di un progetto interamente artistico che cerca di sorprendere attraverso la creazione di spazi inattesi o gratuiti. All'interno della casa si distinguono gli elementi di stile minimalista: cemento, legno, acciaio inossidabile, pareti bianche...

Este apartamento de 300 m² em São Paulo segue o conceito de *design* global: é um projeto inteiramente artístico que procura criar efeitos de surpresa por meio de espaços inesperados ou gratuitos. No interior da casa, destacam-se os elementos do estilo minimalista: betão, madeira, aço inoxidável, paredes brancas, etc.

Denna lägenhet på 300 m² i São Paulo välkomnar idén med övergripande design: det är ett fullständigt konstnärligt projekt som vill överraska genom att skapa oväntade eller oberättigade utrymmen. Inne i huset framträder främst de minimalistiska elementen: betong, trä, rostfritt stål, vita väggar...

In this space, the libraries are integrated into the walls, covering their entire surface.

Les bibliothèques de ce type d'espaces sont intégrées aux murs, couvrant des pans entiers dans la plupart des cas.

Bibliotheken in dieser Art von Räumen integrieren sich in die Mauern und bedecken normalerweise ganze Wände.

Bibliotheken in dit type interieur zijn ingebouwd in de wanden. Meestal bedekken ze de hele muur.

Las bibliotecas de este tipo de espacios se integran en los muros, en la mayoría de los casos cubriendo paredes enteras.

Le biblioteche di questo tipo di spazi si integrano nei muri, nella maggior parte dei casi ricoprendo pareti intere.

As estantes deste tipo de espaços integram-se na parede, cobrindo-a completamente na maior parte dos casos.

Bokhyllor i den här typen av utrymmen brukar integreras i väggen, och i de flesta fall täcker de hela väggen.

Floor plan

MODELO HOUSE

CJ STUDIO // Taipei, Taiwan
© Marc Gerritsen

The design of this apartment is focused on the layout. Different kinds of flooring divide the apartment in two: one area for the kitchen, bathroom, study, and a bedroom; and another that unites the living room, dining room, and master bedroom.

Le design d'intérieur de cet appartement s'est focalisé sur la distribution des espaces. Les différents revêtements au sol permettent de diviser l'appartement en deux : une zone pour la cuisine, la salle de bains, le bureau et une chambre ; une zone qui comporte le salon, la cuisine et la chambre principale.

Das Design im Inneren der Wohnung hat seinen Schwerpunkt auf die Raumverteilung gelegt. Der Gebrauch verschiedener Fußböden teilt den Raum in zwei Wohnungen ein: Eine für die Küche, Badezimmer, Studio und Schlafzimmer; in der anderen befinden sich Wohnzimmer, Esszimmer und Hauptschlafzimmer.

Het interieurontwerp voor dit appartement was gericht op de onderverdeling van de ruimtes. Het gebruik van verschillende soorten vloeren verdeelt het appartement in twee zones: een zone voor de keuken, studio en slaapkamer en een andere zone voor de salon, eetkamer en de grote slaapkamer.

El diseño del interior de este apartamento se ha centrado en la distribución de los espacios. El uso de diferentes pavimentos divide en dos el apartamento: una zona para la cocina, el baño, el estudio y un dormitorio; y otra zona en la que se reúnen el salón, el comedor y el dormitorio principal.

Il progetto dell'interno di questo appartamento si è concentrato sulla distribuzione degli spazi. L'utilizzo di diversi pavimenti divide in due l'appartamento: una zona per la cucina, il bagno, lo studio e una camera da letto; e un'altra zona in cui si racchiudono salone, sala da pranzo e camera da letto principale.

O projeto para o interior deste apartamento centrou-se na distribuição dos espaços. O uso de pavimentos diferentes divide o apartamento em dois: uma zona para a cozinha, casa de banho, escritório e um quarto e outra zona em que se reúnem a sala, a sala de jantar e o quarto principal.

Inredningen i den här lägenheten har fokuserat på fördelningen av utrymmet. Användningen av olika golv delar upp lägenheten i två: ett område med kök, badrum, arbetsrum och sovrum, samt ett område som sammanför vardagsrummet, matsalen och huvudsovrummet.

If the room is large enough, a small auxiliary table may be used behind the sofa or to create separate spaces.

Si la pièce est suffisamment grande, il est possible d'installer une petite table d'appoint à côté du canapé ou pour marquer les différentes ambiances.

Wenn es die Größe der Regale erlaubt, kann ein kleiner Beistelltisch hinter dem Sofa als Raumteiler eingebaut werden.

Als de ruimte in het interieur het toelaat, plaats dan achter de bank een bijzettafeltje om de ruimte in tweeën te delen.

Si la amplitud de la estancia lo permite, se puede instalar una pequeña mesa auxiliar tras el sofá o como separadora de ambientes.

Se la grandezza della stanza lo consente, è possibile inserire un tavolino accessorio dietro al divano o come separatore di ambienti.

Se as dimensões da divisão o permitirem, pode instalar uma pequena mesa de apoio por trás do sofá ou como separadora de ambientes.

Om utrymmet tillåter kan man ställa ett litet bord bakom soffan eller använda det för att separera miljöer.

Floor plan

Using different types of flooring is a good way to separate interior spaces without using partitions.

Une bonne solution pour séparer les espaces sans les cloisonner consiste à utiliser différents types de revêtements à l'intérieur.

Eine geschickte Lösung für die Raumteilung ohne die Errichtung von Trennwänden liegt im Einbau verschiedener Fußböden in den Innenräumen.

Een goede oplossing om ruimtes van elkaar te scheiden zonder wanden te plaatsen, is verschillende soorten vloeren gebruiken.

Una buena solución para separar espacios sin levantar tabiques es utilizar diferentes tipos de pavimento en el interior.

Una buona soluzione per separare gli spazi senza erigere tramezzi è utilizzare tipi di pavimento diversi negli interni.

Uma boa solução para separar espaços sem erguer paredes consiste em utilizar diversos tipos de pavimento no interior.

En bra lösning för att skilja fria utrymmen åt utan att sätta upp rumsavdelare är att använda olika typer av golv.

LUDWIG PENTHOUSE

CRAIG STEELY ARCHITECTURE // San Francisco, CA, USA
© Tim Griffith

The original layout of this apartment was modified, opening spaces to the outside to moderate its temperature, which was too hot on the south side. The result is natural air conditioning that not only contributes to the reduction of CO_2 but also reduces energy consumption.

L'agencement d'origine de l'appartement a été modifié afin d'ouvrir les espaces sur l'extérieur et ainsi équilibrer la température totale de l'appartement dont la façade sud était trop exposée à la chaleur. Il en résulte une climatisation naturelle bien plus durable qui contribue à la réduction des émissions de CO_2 et de la consommation.

Die ursprüngliche Raumverteilung dieser Wohnung wurde verändert und öffnet sich nach außen, um somit die Gesamttemperatur der Wohnung auszugleichen, bei der die Südfassade zu viel geheizt wurde. Das Ergebnis ist eine natürliche Klimatisierung, die weit nachhaltiger ist, da sie den CO_2 Ausstoß verringert und am Energieverbrauch spart.

De originele indeling van het appartement werd opengebroken om de ruimtes meer naar buiten toe te openen en om de temperatuur, die te veel bepaald werd door de zonnige zuidkant, gelijkmatiger te verdelen. Het resultaat is een natuurlijke klimaatregeling die veel duurzamer is, die bijdraagt aan de vermindering van CO_2-uitstoot en die energie bespaart.

La distribución original del apartamento se modificó para abrir los espacios al exterior y así equilibrar la temperatura global del apartamento, que se calentaba demasiado en la fachada sur. El resultado es una climatización natural mucho más sostenible que contribuye a la reducción de CO_2 y a un ahorro en el consumo.

La distribuzione originale dell'appartamento è stata modificata per aprire gli spazi verso l'esterno ed equilibrare in questo modo la temperatura complessiva dell'appartamento, che si riscaldava troppo in corrispondenza della facciata sud. Il risultato è una climatizzazione naturale molto più sostenibile, che contribuisce alla riduzione di CO_2 e a un risparmio nel consumo.

A divisão original deste apartamento foi alterada de modo a abrir os espaços para o exterior e equilibrar, desse modo, a temperatura global do apartamento, que aquecia demasiado na fachada sul. O resultado é uma climatização natural, muito mais sustentável, que contribui para a redução do CO_2 e para uma poupança no consumo.

Den ursprungliga utformningen av lägenheten ändrades för att öppna upp mot utsidan och därmed balansera den totala temperaturen i lägenheten, som blev för varm av den södra fasaden. Resultatet är ett mycket mer hållbart naturligt klimat som bidrar till att minska utsläppen av CO_2 och sparar pengar för konsumenten.

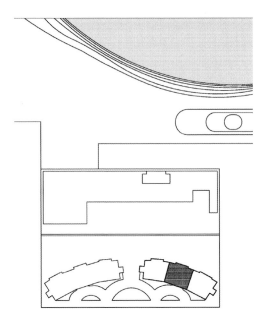

Site plan

Floor plan

Environmental responsibility is shown by the use in these finishes of fine walnut from trees that have fallen naturally.

La responsabilité environnementale se dénote dans l'usage de matériaux nobles, comme le bois de noyer déjà tombé utilisé dans les revêtements.

Die Zuständigkeit der Umwelt macht sich in den eleganten Materialien wie Nussbaumholz bemerkbar, das schon in der Verkleidung verwendet wurde.

Een milieubewuste keuze is bijvoorbeeld het gebruik van edele materialen bij de afwerking, zoals verantwoord notenhout.

La responsabilidad medioambiental se nota en el uso de materiales nobles, como la madera de nogal ya caído utilizada en los revestimientos.

La responsabilità ambientale si nota nell'uso di materiali nobili, come il legno di noce già caduto utilizzato per i rivestimenti.

A responsabilidade ambiental é revelada pelo uso de materiais nobres, como a madeira de nogueira caída utilizada nos revestimentos.

Miljömedvetenheten är tydlig i användningen av ädla material, som valnötsträ från redan fallna träd som golv.

The master bedroom and bathroom are fused in a single space. Partitions have been eliminated, producing a more spacious room.

La chambre et la salle de bains principale ne forment plus qu'un seul et même espace. Les cloisons ont été supprimées pour obtenir une pièce plus vaste.

Die Hauptschlaf- und Badezimmer vereinen sich in einem einzigen Raum. Die Aufteilung wird aufgehoben und ein größerer Raum geschaffen.

De slaapkamer en de grote badkamer vormen één geheel. Partities zijn weggehaald om een grotere ruimte te creëren

El dormitorio y el baño principal se fusionan en un único espacio. Se eliminan las particiones y se logra una estancia más amplia.

La camera da letto e il bagno principale si fondono in un unico spazio. Sono eliminate le separazioni e si ottiene una stanza più grande.

O quarto e a casa de banho principal fundem-se num único espaço. Eliminando as divisórias, consegue-se uma divisão mais ampla.

Sovrummet och det stora badrummet slås samman till en enda plats. Man har tagit bort väggarna och fått ett mycket större rum.

LOFT IN HAMBURG

GRAFT GESELLSCHAFT VON ARCHITEKTEN // Hamburg, Germany
© Ricardo Ridecos

The spaces in this apartment are arranged around an attractive walnut module that is far from conventional partitions. The combination of pale-coloured peripheral features and furniture generates a dynamic feeling.

Les espaces de cet appartement ont été agencés autour d'un module en noyer plutôt voyant qui brise les cloisonnements conventionnels et les divisions classiques. La combinaison de couleurs et de tons clairs au niveau des éléments et des meubles périphériques apporte une touche de dynamisme.

Die Organisation der Räume dieses Appartements wird durch ein auffälliges Modul aus Walnussholz realisiert, das mit den konventionellen Aufteilern und regulären Trennungen bricht. Die Farbkombination aus klaren Farben in den peripheen Elementen und Möbeln schafft Dynamik.

De indeling van het appartement wordt gerealiseerd door een opvallende module van notenhout die de conventionele afscheidingen en gebruikelijke verdeling doorbreekt. De combinatie van heldere kleuren voor de elementen en het meubilair eromheen creëert een dynamische sfeer.

La organización de los espacios de este apartamento se realiza alrededor de un llamativo módulo de madera de nogal que rompe con las particiones convencionales y las divisiones regulares. La combinación de colores, de tonos claros, en los elementos y los muebles periféricos genera dinamismo.

L'organizzazione degli spazi di questo appartamento si produce attorno a un vistoso modulo di legno di noce che rompe con le separazioni convenzionali e le divisioni regolari. La combinazione di colori dalle tonalità chiare, negli elementi e nei mobili periferici genera dinamismo.

A organização dos espaços deste apartamento é efetuada em redor de um atraente módulo em madeira de nogueira, que rompe com as distribuições convencionais e as divisões regulares. A combinação das cores de tons claros nos elementos e nos móveis periféricos gera um efeito dinâmico.

Fördelningen av utrymmen i denna lägenhet har skett kring en slående modul i valnöt som bryter mot konventionella rumsdelare och väggar. Kombinationen av färger i ljusa nyanser utgör perifera inslag och möbler genererar dynamik.

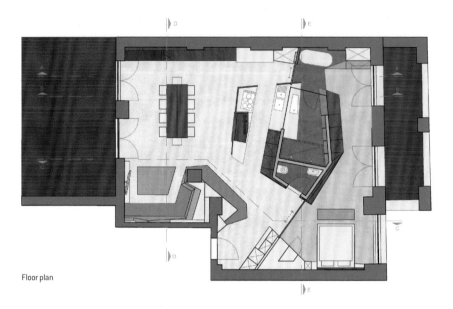

Floor plan

Multipurpose modules can be used to reorganize spaces and transition zones.

La construction de modules multifonctions est une bonne solution, car ils permettent de réorganiser les espaces et les zones de passage.

Der Bau von Modulen mit verschiedenen Funktionen ist eine gute Lösung, da sie die Räume neu ordnen und Zirkulation schaffen.

De constructie van multifunctionele modules is een goede oplossing voor een betere indeling en doorlooruimte.

La construcción de módulos con varias funciones es una buena solución, ya que reorganizan los espacios y las áreas de circulación.

La costruzione di moduli con varie funzioni è una buona soluzione, poiché riorganizzano gli spazi e le aree di circolazione.

A construção de módulos multifuncionais é uma boa solução, uma vez que reorganizam os espaços e as áreas de circulação.

Konstruktion av moduler med olika funktioner är en bra lösning, eftersom det omorganiserar bostaden och umgängesytorna.

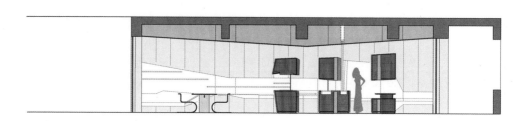

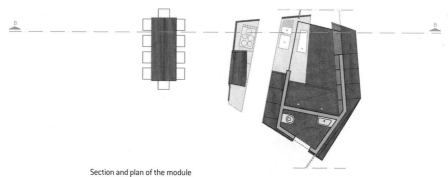

Section and plan of the module

A minimalist space can also be a blended space. This module unites the kitchen, bathroom, a library, and a storage area.

Un espace minimaliste est aussi synonyme de fusion des espaces. Ce module conjugue la cuisine, la salle d'eau, une bibliothèque et un espace de stockage.

Ein minimalistischer Ort ist auch der, der den Raum verschmelzen lässt. Dieses Modul vereint Küche, Badezimmer, Bibliothek und Stauraum.

Een minimalistische ruimte is meestal een samengestelde ruimte. Deze module biedt onderdak aan de keuken, de badkamer, een bibliotheek en een berging.

Un espacio minimalista es también aquel que logra un espacio fusionado. Este módulo reúne la cocina, el baño, una librería y un área de almacenamiento.

Uno spazio minimalista è anche quello che combina gli spazi. Questo modulo comprende la cucina, il bagno, una libreria e un'area ripostiglio.

Um espaço minimalista é também aquele que consegue um espaço fusionado. Este módulo reúne a cozinha, a casa de banho, uma estante e uma zona de arrumação.

Minimalistiskt är det också med utrymmen som slås ihop. Den här modulen slår samman kök, badrum, bibliotek och förvaring.

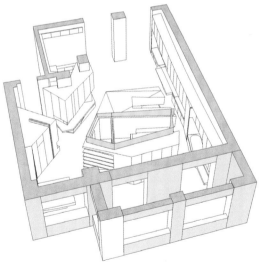

Axonometric of the open module

APARTMENT IN WULUMUQI STREET

SCISKEWCOLLABORATIVE // Shanghai, China
© Courtesy of sciskewcollaborative

The roof of the building was raised and a glass skylight installed to provide more light. The shapes of the roof and the staircase to the mezzanine are the most distinctive features here. Overlapping of the pieces generates spatial movement.

Une fois le toit de l'édifice surélevé, il a été possible d'installer une lucarne en verre pour obtenir plus de lumière naturelle. La forme du plafond et celle de l'escalier qui mène à la mezzanine sont les éléments les plus marquants de ce lieu. La superposition des pièces crée un mouvement dans l'espace.

Nach der Erhebung des Daches konnte eine Dachluke aus Glas eingebaut werden, um mehr Licht zu erhalten. Die Formen der Decke und Treppe, die in das Zwischengeschoss führt, sind das Erkennungsmerkmal des Gesamtkomplexes. Die Übereinanderlagerung der Stücke schafft räumliche Bewegung.

Door het dak van het gebouw te verhogen, kon er een glazen koepel geplaatst worden die ervoor zorgt dat het licht maximaal opgevangen wordt. De vorm van het dak en die van de trap naar de tussenverdieping zijn de meest onderscheidende elementen in de woning. Het boven elkaar plaatsen van elementen creëert beweging en ruimte.

Tras elevar la cubierta del edificio se pudo instalar una claraboya de cristal para conseguir una mayor entrada de luz. La forma del techo y la de la escalera que lleva a la entreplanta son el elemento más distintivo del conjunto de la vivienda. La superposición de las piezas genera movimiento espacial.

Dopo aver alzato il tetto dell'edificio, è stato possibile installare un lucernario di vetro per ottenere un maggiore ingresso di luce. La forma del soffitto e della scala che porta al piano rialzato sono gli elementi più distintivi dell'insieme della casa. La sovrapposizione delle parti genera movimento spaziale.

Depois de ter elevado a cobertura do edifício, foi possível instalar uma claraboia de vidro, que permite uma maior entrada de luz. A forma do teto e a da escada que conduz ao andar intermédio constituem o elemento distintivo de todo o conjunto da casa. A sobreposição de peças gera um movimento espacial.

Efter att taket höjts kunde man installera ett stort takfönster till, för att ge större ljuspenetrering. Formen på taket och trappan som leder till mellanvåningen är de mest säregna delarna ihela huset. De överlappande trappstegen ger en känsla av rörelse i rummet.

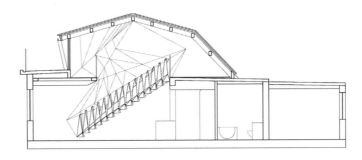

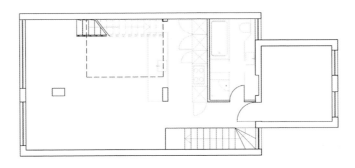

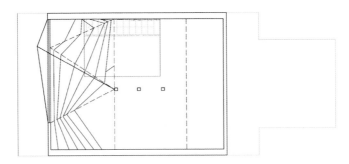

Section and floor plans

Unified spaces that play several roles offer less privacy, but better sight lines and luminosity.

En combinant plusieurs fonctions, les espaces unifiés réduisent l'intimité mais améliorent la perspective d'ensemble et la luminosité.

Die vereinten Räume bieten weniger Privatsphäre, da sie mehrere Funktionen haben, aber verbessern die gesamte Wahrnehmung und Beleuchtung.

Gedeelde, multifunctionele ruimtes hebben minder privacy, maar hebben het voordeel van betere zichtlijnen en mooier binnenvallend licht.

Los espacios unificados restan privacidad al compartir varias funciones, pero mejoran la percepción global y la iluminación.

Gli spazi uniti tolgono privacy perché condividono varie funzioni, ma migliorano la percezione complessiva e l'illuminazione

Embora reduzam a privacidade, uma vez que asseguram diversas funções, os espaços unificados melhoram a perceção global e a iluminação.

Sammanslagna rum går miste om avskildhet på vissa sätt, men förbättrar det övergripande intrycket och belysningen.

Combine light textures and materials. The use of white, the wooden floors, and the bathroom stone are ideally suited to this minimalist design.

Combinez des textures et des matériaux légers. Dans ce cas, le blanc, le bois du sol et la pierre de la salle de bains sont en adéquation totale dans cet environnement minimaliste.

Kombinieren Sie leichte Strukturen und Materialien. In diesem Fall passen sich die weiße Farbe, das Holz des Fußbodens und die Steinfliesen im Badezimmer optimal an die minimalistische Umgebung an.

Werk met transparante texturen en materialen. Hier dragen witte muren, houten vloeren en het licht sanitair in de badkamer bij aan een minimalistische sfeer.

Combina texturas y materiales livianos. En este caso, el blanco, la madera del suelo y la piedra del baño se adaptan perfectamente a este ambiente minimalista.

Abbina trame e materiali leggeri. In questo caso il bianco, il legno del pavimento e la pietra del bagno si adattano perfettamente a questo ambiente minimalista.

Combine texturas e materiais leves. Neste caso, o branco, o chão de madeira e a pedra da casa de banho adaptam-se perfeitamente a este ambiente minimalista.

Kombinera enkla texturer och material. I det här fallet smälter det vita, träet i golvet och stenen i badrummet samman perfekt i den minimalistiska miljön.

KANG DUPLEX

CJ STUDIO // Taipei, Taiwan
© Kuomin Lee

This duplex was inspired by origami. Its elongated and narrow floor plan was poorly lit, so the back wall of the house was replaced by frosted glass, while the other walls and the ceiling were painted white in accordance with a minimalist aesthetic.

Ce duplex est inspiré de la pratique de l'origami. Sa superficie longue et étroite ne permettait pas d'avoir un bon éclairage. Pour pallier cela, le mur de la façade arrière a été remplacé par du verre poli. Les murs ainsi que le plafond ont aussi été peints en blanc, en accord avec l'esthétique minimaliste de l'ensemble.

Dieses Duplex ist von der *Origami* Praxis inspiriert worden. Sein länglicher und schmaler Grundriss begünstigt nicht gerade die Beleuchtung. Um diesen Aspekt zu verbessern, wurde die Wand der hinteren Fassade durch eine aus mattem Glas ersetzt. Die Decke wurde weiß angemalt, was zur minimalistischen Ästhetik des Gesamtkomplexes passt.

Deze duplex is geïnspireerd op de origamitechniek. De langgerekte en smalle benedenverdieping kreeg niet voldoende licht. Daarom werd de achtergevel van de woning vervangen door een matglazen wand en werden de muren en het dak wit geverfd, conform de minimalistische esthetiek van het geheel.

Este dúplex está inspirado en la práctica del *origami*. Su planta alargada y estrecha no favorece una buena iluminación. Para mejorar este aspecto, se sustituyó la pared de la fachada trasera por cristal esmerilado y las paredes y el techo se pintaron de blanco, de acuerdo con la estética minimalista del conjunto.

Questo duplex trae ispirazione dalla pratica dell'*origami*. La sua pianta allungata e stretta non favorisce una buona illuminazione. Per migliorare questo aspetto, è stata sostituita la parete della facciata posteriore con vetro smerigliato, e le pareti e il soffitto sono stati tinteggiati di bianco, mantenendo l'estetica minimalista dell'insieme.

Este duplex inspira-se na técnica do *origami*. A sua planta alongada e estreita não favorece uma boa iluminação. Para obviar a este inconveniente, a parede da fachada das traseiras foi substituída por vidro esmerilado e as paredes e teto foram pintados de branco, de acordo com a estética minimalista do conjunto.

Denna tvårummare är inspirerad av *origami*. Den långa och smala formen underlättar inte för bra belysning. För att förbättra det ersatte man väggen på den bakre fasaden med frostat glas och väggar och tak målades vita, i enlighet med den övergripande minimalistiska estetiken.

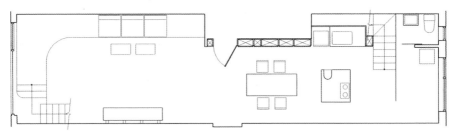

Lower level

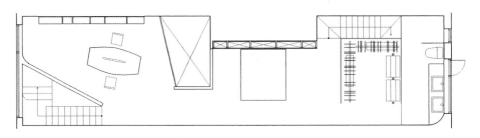

Upper level

To achieve an airy atmosphere, use the same colour range, even when there are different levels.

Pour obtenir un espace épuré, il est préférable d'utiliser la même gamme chromatique, y compris sur différents niveaux.

Um eine durchscheinende Umgebung zu schaffen, sollte man eine einheitliche Farbpalette wählen, auch wenn verschiedene Ebenen existieren.

Om een licht en transparant interieur te creëren, is het aan te raden hetzelfde kleurenpalet toe te passen op alle niveaus.

Para conseguir un ambiente diáfano es recomendable utilizar la misma gama cromática, incluso cuando existen niveles diferentes.

Per ottenere un ambiente chiaro è consigliabile utilizzare la stessa gamma cromatica, anche quando sono presenti livelli differenti.

Para conseguir um ambiente transparente, é recomendável utilizar a mesma paleta cromática, mesmo quando existem diversos andares.

För att få en genomskinlig miljö är det bra att använda samma färgskala, även mellan olika våningsplan.

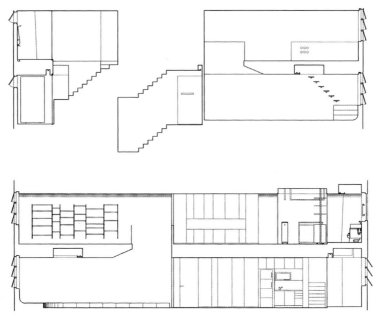

Sections

The design of stairs can improve the lighting in upstairs rooms.

L'installation d'un escalier peut être une bonne opportunité d'améliorer l'éclairage des pièces du niveau supérieur.

Der Einbau von Treppen kann der Optimierung der Beleuchtung in den oberen Stockwerken dienen.

Een trap kan een goede optie zijn om ervoor te zorgen dat de kamers boven ook voldoende licht krijgen.

La instalación de escaleras puede ser una buena oportunidad para mejorar la iluminación de las estancias del nivel superior.

L'installazione di scale può essere una buona possibilità per migliorare l'illuminazione delle stanze del livello superiore.

A instalação das escadas pode constituir uma boa oportunidade para melhorar a iluminação das divisões do andar de cima.

Installation av en trappa kan vara ett bra sätt att förbättra belysningen på övervåningen.

WHITE APARTMENT

PARASITE STUDIO // Timisoara, Romania
© Andrei Margulescu, Parasite Studio

The owners of this apartment wanted to break away from conventional interior design without sacrificing elegance, flexibility, or functionality. White was used as the base on which to superimpose furniture that was treated as a single piece.

Les propriétaires de cet appartement désiraient s'éloigner du design d'intérieur conventionnel mais sans renoncer à l'élégance, la flexibilité et la fonctionnalité des espaces. La couleur blanche a constitué la toile de fond sur laquelle le mobilier a été inséré, constituant un élément à part entière.

Die Besitzer dieser Wohnung wollten sich von dem konventionellen Innendesign verabschieden, aber ohne dabei die Eleganz, die Flexibilität und Funktionalität zu zerstören. Die weiße Farbe wurde als Basis gewählt, um darauf das Mobiliar anzurichten, das wie ein Einzelwerk wirkt.

De eigenaren van dit appartement wilden iets anders dan een conventioneel interieurontwerp, maar wilden geen concessies doen aan de elegantie, veelzijdigheid en functionaliteit van de ruimtes. Wit werd als basis genomen en de meubels werden daarop afgestemd, zodat alles één geheel vormt.

Los propietarios de este apartamento querían alejarse del diseño de interiores convencional, pero sin renunciar a la elegancia, la flexibilidad y la funcionalidad de los espacios. El color blanco se tomó como base sobre la que insertar el mobiliario, tratado como una pieza unitaria.

I proprietari di questo appartamento volevano prendere le distanze dal design d'interni convenzionale, ma senza rinunciare a eleganza, flessibilità e funzionalità degli spazi. Il colore bianco è stato preso come base su cui inserire i mobili, trattati come un pezzo unico.

Os proprietários deste apartamento queriam afastar-se do *design* convencional de interiores, mas sem renunciar à elegância, à flexibilidade e à funcionalidade dos espaços. A cor branca foi selecionada como base para a colocação do mobiliário, tratado como uma peça unitária.

Ägarna av lägenheten ville undvika konventionell inredning, men utan att offra elegans, flexibilitet och funktionalitet i rummen. Den vita färgen användes som en grund för möblerna, och sågs som en egen inredningsdetalj.

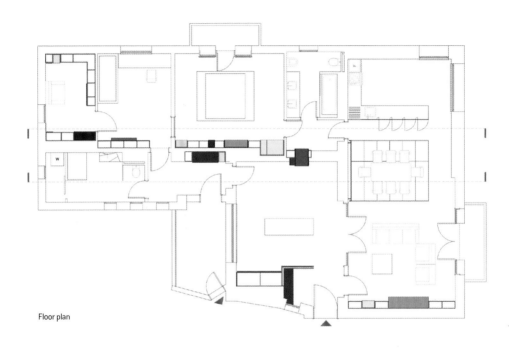

Floor plan

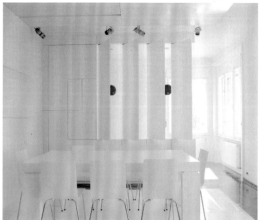

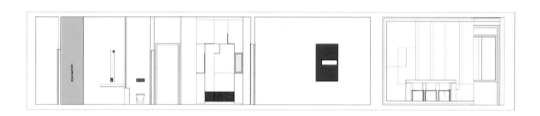

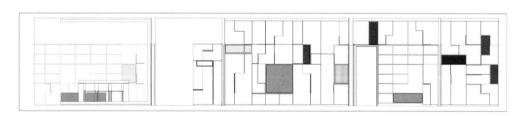

Sections

The kitchen is separated from the dining room by hanging white movable panels, which allow light to enter.

La cuisine est séparée de la salle à manger grâce à quelques panneaux amovibles de couleur blanche permettant de laisser entrer la lumière.

Die Küche wird vom Esszimmer durch einige kippbare weiße Paneelen, die das Licht durchdringen lassen, abgetrennt.

De keuken is afgescheiden van de eetkamer door witte kieppanelen die het licht binnenlaten.

La cocina se separa del comedor gracias a unos paneles basculantes de color blanco que permiten la entrada de luz.

La cucina è separata dalla sala da pranzo grazie a dei pannelli basculanti di colore bianco che favoriscono l'ingresso della luce.

A cozinha está separada da sala de jantar por meio de painéis basculantes de cor branca, que permitem a entrada da luz.

Köket är avskilt från matsalen genom vändbara vita paneler som släpper in ljus.

Furnish your bedroom with made-to-measure furniture. Geometric shapes and accent colours break up the monotonous white.

Décorez votre chambre avec du mobilier sur mesure. Les formes géométriques et les touches de couleur brisent la monotonie instaurée par le blanc.

Richten Sie Ihr Schlafzimmer mit Möbeln nach Maß ein. Die geometrischen Formen und farbigen Details brechen mit der Monotonie der weißen Farbe.

Richt je slaapkamer in met op maat gemaakte meubels. De geometrische vormgeving en enkele kleurentoetsen breken de monotonie van de witte basiskleur.

Decora tu dormitorio con mobiliario hecho a medida. Las formas geométricas y las notas de color rompen con la monotonía del blanco.

Decora la tua stanza da letto con mobili fatti su misura. Le forme geometriche e le note di colore spezzano la monotonia del bianco.

Decore o seu quarto com mobiliário feito à medida. As formas geométricas e as notas de cor rompem com a monotonia do branco.

Dekorera ditt sovrum med platsbyggda möbler. Geometriska former och inslag av färg bryter upp det monotont vita.

APARTMENT IN CIUTAT VELLA

YLAB ARQUITECTOS // Barcelona, Spain
© Ciro Frank Schiappa

The main objective in remodelling this building was to maintain its characteristic architectural features—openings with arched frames, wooden beams, and vaulted arches—while transforming the interior into a modern minimalist home.

L'objectif principal de cette rénovation était de préserver les éléments architecturaux caractéristiques de l'édifice – les ouvertures en arc de cercle, les poutres en bois et les plafonds voûtés – tout en transformant l'intérieur en un lieu moderne et minimaliste.

Das Hauptziel dieser Renovierung bestand in der Erhaltung der architektonischen Elemente dieses Gebäudes–Durchgangsnischen, Holzträger und Gewölbebögen– und gleichzeitig im Umbau der Innenräume in eine moderne und minimalistische Wohnung.

De belangrijkste doelstelling bij de renovatie van dit gebouw was het intact houden van de typische architectonische elementen, boogvormige doorgangen en houtwerk, en tegelijkertijd een modern en minimalistisch interieur creëren.

El objetivo principal de esta reforma fue mantener los elementos arquitectónicos característicos del edificio – huecos de paso con arco, vigas de madera y arcos en bovedilla– al tiempo que se transformaba el interior en una vivienda moderna y minimalista.

L'obiettivo principale di questa ristrutturazione è stato quello di mantenere gli elementi architettonici caratteristici dell'edificio –vani di passaggio con arco, travi di legno e archi a volta– e allo stesso tempo trasformare l'interno in una casa moderna e minimalista.

O principal objetivo desta remodelação era a manutenção dos elementos arquitetónicos característicos do edifício – entradas em arco, vigas de madeira e arcos em tijolo – transformando simultaneamente o interior numa residência moderna e minimalista.

Det främsta syftet med denna renovering var att restaurera de arkitektoniska elementen i byggnaden – korridorer med välvda bågar, träbjälkar och välvda tak – samtidigt som man förvandlade interiören till en modern och minimalistisk bostad.

Juxtaposing materials and textures, combined with elegance, can give a unique feel to a space.

La juxtaposition de matériaux et de textures, combinés avec élégance, peut apporter une touche d'originalité à l'espace.

Die Nebeneinanderstellung von elegant verknüpften Materialien und Strukturen bringt Einzigartigkeit.

Het op een verfijnde manier combineren van materialen en texturen geeft karakter aan het interieur.

La yuxtaposición de materiales y texturas, combinados con elegancia, puede dotar de singularidad el ambiente.

L'accostamento di materiali e trame, combinati con eleganza, può rendere singolare l'ambiente.

A justaposição de materiais e texturas, combinados com elegância, pode conferir originalidade ao ambiente.

Mötet mellan material och texturer i kombination med elegans gör rummet unikt.

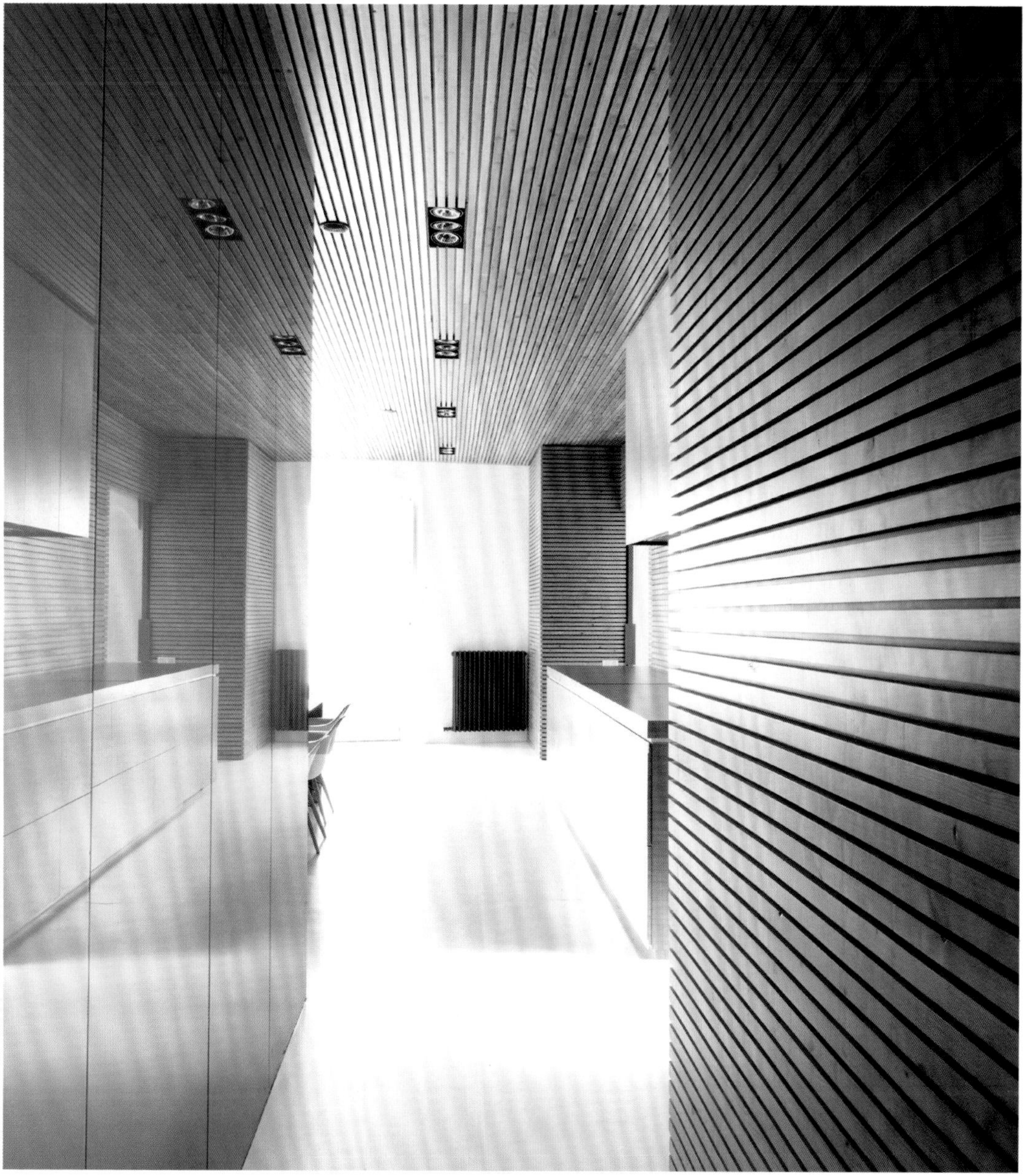

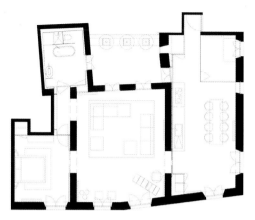

Floor plan

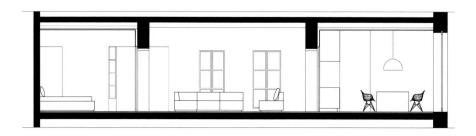

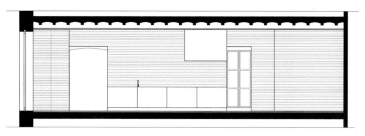

Sections

MORGAN RESIDENCE

TANG KAWASAKI STUDIO // New York, NY, USA
© Björg Magnea

The industrial aesthetic in this Greenwich Village building was maintained inside while minimalist elements were employed to enhance lighting. Radiators and storage modules under the windows have been hidden by encasing them in white wood.

Ce projet a été réalisé dans un édifice industriel de Greenwich Village. L'intérieur conserve une esthétique industrielle avec des éléments minimalistes pour favoriser la luminosité. Sous les fenêtres, les radiateurs ainsi que les modules de stockage ont été masqués par des boiseries blanches pour les cacher aux regards.

Dieses Projekt wurde in dem Industriegebäude Greenwich Village realisiert. Die Innenräume behalten die industrielle Ästhetik bei, mit minimalistischen Elementen, um die Beleuchtung zu begünstigen. Unter den Fenstern wurden in weißer Farbe die Heizungskörper und Stauräume untergebracht und somit fast verborgen.

Dit project werd gerealiseerd in een industrieel gebouw in Greenwich Village, New York. De industriële vormgeving van het pand is behouden en er zijn minimalistische elementen toegevoegd om de lichtinval te verbeteren. Onder de ramen zitten de radiatoren en de opbergruimtes zijn weggewerkt achter een witte betimmering.

Este proyecto se realizó en un edificio industrial de Greenwich Village. El interior mantiene la estética industrial con elementos minimalistas para favorecer la luminosidad. Bajo las ventanas se han cerrado los radiadores y los módulos de almacenaje con carpintería de color blanco, quedando así ocultos.

Questo progetto è stato realizzato in un edificio industriale del Greenwich Village. L'interno mantiene l'estetica industriale con elementi minimalisti per favorire la luminosità. Sotto le finestre sono stati chiusi con serramenti di colore bianco i termosifoni e i moduli per la conservazione, che in questo modo rimangono nascosti.

Este projeto foi realizado num edifício industrial de Greenwich Village. O interior mantém a estética industrial com elementos minimalistas, para favorecer a luminosidade. Por baixo das janelas, os aquecedores e espaços de arrumação foram ocultados por elementos de marcenaria de cor branca.

Det här projektet genomfördes i en industribyggnad i Greenwich Village. Interiören bibehåller det industriella utseendet med minimalistiska inslag för att förbättra ljusstyrkan. Under fönstren har man dolt elementen bakom vita snickerier och förvaringsmoduler.

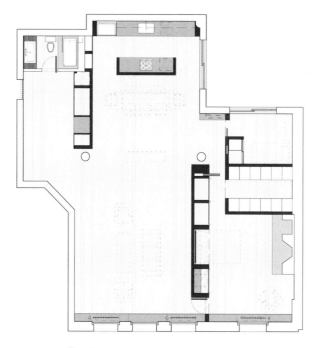

Floor plan

Built-in shelves allow for unobstructed views in open spaces.

Une bonne façon de ne pas entraver la vue au sein des espaces ouverts est d'installer des étagères.

Eine Option, um nicht den Blick nach draußen zu versperren, liegt in der Konstruktion von Einbauregalen.

Een oplossing om de zichtlijnen in een open ruimte open te houden, is een op maat gemaakte wandmeubel te plaatsen.

Una solución para no entorpecer la vista en los espacios abiertos es construir estanterías de obra.

Una soluzione per non ostacolare la vista sugli spazi aperti è quella di costruire scaffali a muro.

Uma solução para não deixar perder a vista em espaços vazios é a construção de estantes embutidas.

En lösning för att undvika att bryta upp synfältet är att bygga in möblerna.

Building a small wall is one of the best ways to hide a kitchen in a loft, especially in a minimalist environment.

L'une des meilleurs solutions pour cacher une cuisine dans un loft, surtout dans un environnement à l'esthétique minimaliste, c'est de faire installer un petit mur.

Wählen Sie die besten Optionen, um die Küche in einem Loft zu verstecken; vor allem in Umgebungen mit minimalistischer Ästhetik sollte eine kleine Mauer gezogen werden.

Een van de beste oplossingen om de keuken uit het zicht te houden in een loft, met name in een minimalistisch interieur, is een laag muurtje te plaatsen.

Una de las mejores soluciones para esconder una cocina en un *loft*, sobre todo en ambientes de estética minimalista, es levantar un pequeño muro.

Una delle soluzioni migliori per nascondere una cucina in un loft, soprattutto in ambienti di estetica minimalista, è quella di erigere un piccolo muro.

Uma das melhores soluções para ocultar a cozinha num *loft*, sobretudo em ambientes de estética minimalista, é levantar um murete.

En av de bästa lösningarna för att dölja ett kök i ett öppet rum, särskilt när man vill ha en minimalistisk estetik, är att sätta upp en liten vägg.

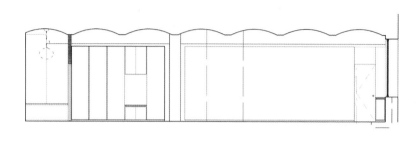

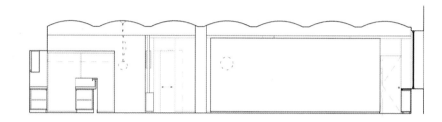

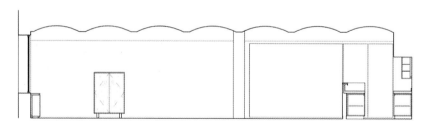

Sections

APARTMENT IN PAMPLONA

ÍÑIGO BEGUIRISTÁIN // Pamplona, Spain
© Iñaki Bergera, www.bergeraphoto.com

This project is an example of how an architect's ingenuity can enrich the overall perception of a space and increase the feeling of spaciousness. Partitions were removed from the communal zone to improve circulation. The private area, on the other hand, is more enclosed to promote relaxation.

Ce projet illustre comment le génie des architectes peut enrichir la perception globale de l'espace et accroître la sensation d'ampleur. Des cloisons ont été supprimées dans la zone commune pour améliorer le passage entre les différents lieux tandis que, dans la zone privée, le cloisonnement des pièces a été conservé pour en préserver le calme.

Dieses Projekt ist ein Beispiel dafür, wie der Erfindergeist eines Architekten die globale Wahrnehmung eines Raumes bereichern und das Gefühl von Weite steigern kann. Das Gemeinschaftszimmer wurde von den Trennwänden befreit, um die Zirkulation zwischen den Bereichen zu verbessern. Der private Bereich dagegen beinhaltet eher verschlossene Ecken, um die Erholung zu gewähren.

Dit project is een voorbeeld van hoe het vernuft van architecten kan bijdragen aan de globale perceptie van een gebouw en aan het gevoel van ruimte. In de gemeenschappelijke zone werden de tussenwanden gesloopt om een betere doorlooopruimte te creëren. In de privézone bleven de kamers meer afgesloten om beter tot rust te kunnen komen.

Este proyecto es un ejemplo de cómo el ingenio de los arquitectos puede enriquecer la percepción global del espacio e incrementar la sensación de amplitud. La zona común se liberó de tabiques para mejorar la circulación entre ámbitos. La zona privada, en cambio, se mantiene con estancias más cerradas para favorecer el descanso.

Questo progetto è un esempio di come l'ingegno degli architetti possa arricchire la percezione complessiva dello spazio e aumentare la sensazione di ampiezza. La zona comune è stata liberata da tramezzi per migliorare la circolazione tra gli ambienti. La zona privata, invece, mantiene stanze più chiuse per favorire il riposo.

Este projeto é um exemplo de como o engenho dos arquitetos pode enriquecer a perceção global do espaço e intensificar a sensação de amplitude. A área comum foi libertada de divisórias, para facilitar a circulação entre as diversas zonas. Na área privada, pelo contrário, optou-se por divisões mais fechadas, mais adequadas ao repouso.

Det här projektet är ett exempel på hur uppfinningsrikedom hos arkitekterna kan förbättra den övergripande uppfattningen om utrymmet och öka känslan av rymd. Den gemensamma zonen befrias från väggar för att förbättra cirkulationen mellan delarna. Den privata zonen får emellertid kvarstå som enskilda rum för att främja avkopplingen.

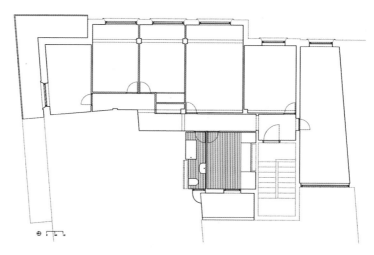

Floor plan before the refurbishment

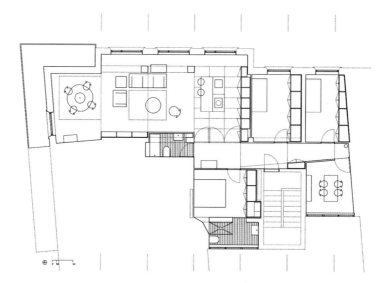

Floor plan after the refurbishment

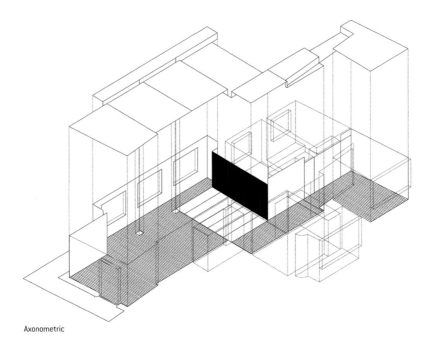

Axonometric

Arrange the interior according to necessity. In this case daytime-use areas have been united in a single space, separate from the bedrooms.

Agencez votre intérieur en fonction de vos besoins. Dans ce cas, les pièces à vivre, formant un seul et même espace, ont été séparées des chambres.

Verteilen Sie den Innenbereich nach Ihren Bedürfnissen In diesem Fall wurden die Tageszonen, die alle in einem Raum liegen, von den Schlafzimmern getrennt.

Maak naar behoefte een indeling van het interieur. Hier worden de dagruimtes, alle ondergebracht in één grote ruimte, afgescheiden van de slaapkamers.

Distribuye el interior en función de las necesidades. En este caso se han separado las zonas de día, ubicadas en único espacio, de los dormitorios.

Distribuisci gli interni in funzione delle esigenze. In questo caso sono state separate le zone giorno, collocate in un unico spazio, dalle stanze da letto.

Proceda à distribuição de espaços interiores em função das necessidades. Neste caso, separaram-se as zonas de dia, localizadas num espaço único, dos quartos.

Fördela inredningen efter behovet. I det här fallet har man skilt dagsutrymmena, som ligger i ett rum, från sovrummen.

Natural light is a great ally in small spaces such as bathrooms. In this case, a white blind ensures that light can enter.

La lumière naturelle est une alliée de premier plan pour les petites pièces comme pour les salles d'eau. Ici, un store blanc assure l'entrée de la lumière.

Die natürliche Beleuchtung ist ein großer Verbündeter der kleineren Räume, wie der Badezimmer. In diesem Fall garantiert ein weißes Rollo das Eindringen von Licht.

Kleine ruimtes, zoals de badkamer, houden van natuurlijk licht. Hier zorgt een wit rolgordijn ervoor dat het natuurlijk licht naar binnen kan schijnen.

La iluminación natural es una gran aliada en las estancias pequeñas como los baños. En este caso, un estor blanco garantiza la entrada de luz.

L'illuminazione naturale è una grande alleata nelle stanze piccole come i bagni. In questo caso, una tenda bianca garantisce l'ingresso di luce.

A iluminação natural é uma grande aliada em divisões pequenas, como as casas de banho. Neste caso, o estore branco garante a entrada da luz.

Naturligt ljus är till stor nytta i små rum, som badrum. I det här fallet gör en tunn vit rullgardin att ljuset garanterat kommer in.

CONNOR RESIDENCE

EMILIO FUSCALDO, IMOGEN PULLAR / NEST ARCHITECTS // Elwood, Australia
© Jesse Marlow

A minimalist approach in the interior of this apartment creates a cosy and restful atmosphere. Items of furniture are active features of the home, framing the visual and austere aesthetic.

Le design intérieur de cet appartement a été conçu selon un critère minimaliste pour créer un environnement accueillant et posé. Les pièces du mobilier s'apparentent à des éléments actifs de l'habitat, définissant une esthétique visuelle au sein d'un ensemble épuré.

Die Innenräume der Wohnung wurden nach minimalistischen Kriterien entworfen, um somit ein gemütliches und ruhiges Ambiente zu schaffen. Die Möbelstücke handeln wie aktive Elemente der Wohnung. Sie verdeutlichen die visuelle Ästhetik in dieser einfachen Einheit.

Het interieur van dit appartement is ontworpen volgens minimalistische criteria. Zo ontstaat een gezellige en rustige sfeer. De meubelstukken worden ingezet als visuele aandachtstrekkers in een verder sober ogend geheel.

Los interiores de este apartamento se han diseñado bajo un criterio minimalista para crear un ambiente acogedor y pausado. Las piezas de mobiliario actúan como elementos activos de la vivienda, marcando la estética visual dentro del austero conjunto.

Gli interni di questo appartamento sono stati progettati secondo un criterio minimalista per creare un ambiente accogliente e tranquillo. I pezzi di arredamento si comportano come elementi attivi della casa, marcando l'estetica visuale all'interno dell'insieme austero.

Os interiores deste apartamento foram projetados segundo um critério minimalista, para criar um ambiente acolhedor e sereno. As peças de mobiliário funcionam como elementos ativos da casa, marcando a estética visual no seio do austero conjunto.

Interiören i denna lägenhet har designats enligt minimalistiska kriterier för att skapa en mysig och lugn miljö. Möblerna fungerar som aktiva inslag i huset och markerar husets strama visuella estetik.

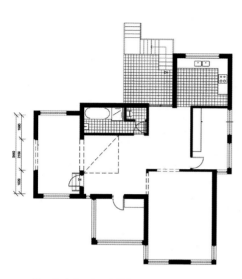

Floor plan before the refurbishment

Floor plan after the refurbishment

If you decide to remodel your home, remember that visual pathways can be used to make spaces more airy and comfortable.

Si vous décidez de réagencer votre espace de vie, valorisez les perspectives afin de créer des espaces plus confortables et plus lumineux.

Wenn Sie Ihre Wohnung umbauen wollen, beachten Sie die visuellen Durchgänge, um einen noch komfortableren und durchsichtigeren Raum zu schaffen.

Als je je huis anders wilt inrichten, houd dan rekening met de zichtlijnen om een comfortabel en overzichtelijk interieur te creëren.

Si decides remodelar tu vivienda ten en cuenta los recorridos visuales para crear espacios más confortables y diáfanos.

Se decidi di ristrutturare la tua casa, fai attenzione ai percorsi visivi per creare spazi più confortevoli e chiari.

Se decidir remodelar a sua casa, tenha em consideração os percursos visuais, a fim de criar espaços mais confortáveis e transparentes.

Om du bestämmer dig för att renovera ditt hem ska du ta hänsyn till synvägarna för att skapa mer bekväma och luftiga utrymmen.

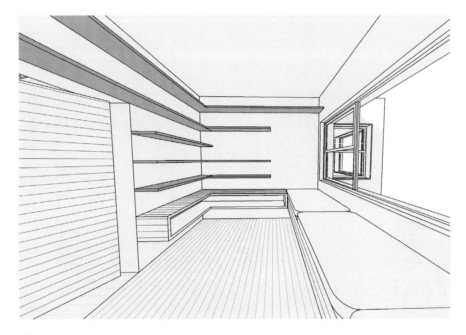

3-D representation

LOFT IN EIXAMPLE

DATA AE // Barcelona, Spain
© René Pedersen

This compact space integrates different uses in a single, luminous volume where partitions have been removed and a flowing multipurpose structure has been installed. Light and simple lines are the dominant features.

L'objectif principal était d'intégrer différentes fonctionnalités dans un volume compact afin d'obtenir un espace fluide. Il se présente comme un tout lumineux : les cloisons ont été supprimées pour donner lieu à une structure combinant différentes utilités. La lumière et des lignes simples en sont les éléments prédominants.

Das Hauptziel lag in der Eingliederung der verschiedenen Verwendungen in ein kompaktes Volumen, um einen Raumfluss zu ermöglichen. Der Raum ist wie ein helles Ganzes, aus dem die Trennwände entfernt wurden und eine Struktur hineingebaut wurde, die verschiedene Dienste vereint. Licht und einfache Linien sind die vorherrschenden Elemente.

De belangrijkste doelstelling was de verschillende toepassingen samen te brengen in een compacte, vloeiende ruimte. Het is een lichtdoorlatende ruimte zonder tussenwanden geworden en er is een structuur aangebracht die multifunctioneel is. De voornaamste elementen zijn licht en eenvoudige lijnen.

El objetivo principal fue integrar los diferentes usos en un volumen compacto para conseguir que el espacio fluya. El espacio se presenta como un todo luminoso, en el que se han eliminado los tabiques y se ha colocado una estructura que reúne varios servicios. Luz y líneas simples son los elementos predominantes.

L'obiettivo principale è stato quello di integrare i vari usi in un volume compatto per ottenere uno spazio che fluisca. Lo spazio si presenta come un intero luminoso, in cui sono stati eliminati i tramezzi ed è stata sistemata una struttura che riunisce i vari servizi. Luce e linee semplici sono gli elementi dominanti.

O objetivo principal era integrar as diferentes utilizações num volume compacto, de forma a fazer fluir o espaço. O espaço apresenta-se como um todo luminoso, em que foram eliminadas todas as divisórias e onde foi integrada uma estrutura que reúne vários serviços. Luz e linhas simples são os elementos predominantes.

Det främsta målet var att integrera de olika användningsområdena i en kompakt volym för att ge utrymmet flöde. Utrymmet presenteras som en enda stort ljus, där skiljeväggarna har avlägsnats och man har ställt in en struktur som förenar olika funktioner. Ljus och enkla linjer är de dominerande elementen.

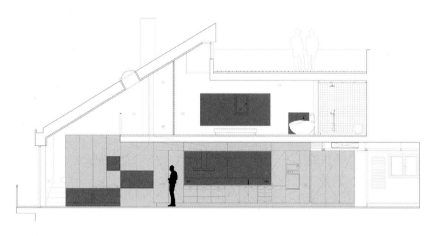

Section

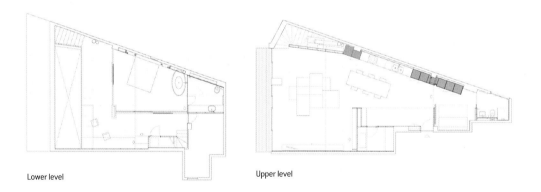

Lower level

Upper level

Although open spaces are prevalent in minimalist layouts, leave room for a degree of privacy.

Même si les espaces ouverts prédominent dans un agencement minimaliste, il est recommandé de préserver un certain degré d'intimité.

Obwohl in einer minimalistischen Aufteilung der offene Raum dominiert, sollte man Platz für Intimität lassen.

Hoewel in een minimalistische indeling de ruimtes open blijven, is het raadzaam ook plaats te reserveren voor een beetje intimiteit.

Aunque en una distribución minimalista prevalecen los espacios abiertos, es recomendable dejar margen para cierta intimidad.

Anche se in una distribuzione minimalista prevalgono gli spazi aperti, è consigliabile lasciare un margine per un po' d'intimità.

Embora numa distribuição minimalista os espaços abertos predominem, é conveniente deixar margem para uma certa intimidade.

Även om en minimalistisk distribution oftast råder i öppna rum är det lämpligt att lämna utrymme för viss avskildhet.

Mobile partitions that use light materials can be moved easily. If they are permanent, translucent materials are preferable.

Les cloisons amovibles doivent être composées de matériaux légers afin de les déplacer facilement. Si ces cloisons ne sont pas amovibles, il est préférable qu'elles soient faites de matériaux translucides.

Die beweglichen Raumteiler sollten aus leichtem Material und schnell zu verschieben sein. Wenn sie permanent sind, sollte man eher zu durchsichtigen Materialien greifen.

Mobiele partities moeten van licht materiaal zijn om ze makkelijk te verplaatsen. Vaste partities kunnen beter van doorschijnend materiaal zijn.

Las particiones móviles deben construirse con materiales ligeros que permitan moverlas fácilmente. Si son permanentes, son preferibles materiales translúcidos.

Le separazioni mobili devono essere costruite con materiali leggeri che consentano di muoverle agevolmente. Se sono permanenti, sono da preferire i materiali traslucidi.

As divisórias móveis devem ser construídas com materiais leves, que permitam movê-las facilmente. Se forem permanentes, são preferíveis os materiais translúcidos.

Flyttbara skiljeväggar ska vara byggde i lättviktsmaterial så att det blir enkelt att flytta dem. Om de är permanenta är genomskinliga material att föredra.

HOUSE-STUDIO IN RAVAL

AGUSTÍ COSTA // Barcelona, Spain
© David Cardelús

This interior had to house a workspace as well as living space. The owner's open-mindedness was a boon to the architect, enabling him to propose an uninhibited plan with maximum visual interaction between rooms.

Cet intérieur devait comporter un espace de travail et un espace de vie. La propriétaire étant sans complexe, l'architecte a opté pour une grande fenêtre et a pu réaliser un projet tout aussi dénué d'inhibitions, où les pièces sont reliées avec une interaction visuelle maximale.

Dieser Innenraum sollte den Arbeitsplatz mit dem Wohnraum verbinden. Die Besitzerin kannte keine Hemmungen, was ein großer Vorteil für den Architekten darstellte, der ein ungezwungenes Projekt starten konnte, bei dem die Beziehung zwischen den Räumen die größte visuelle Wechselwirkung ermöglicht.

Het interieur is een combinatie van een werk- en woonruimte. De eigenares is een vrijdenkende vrouw en dat was voor de architect een groot voordeel. Hij maakte er een gewaagd project van waarbij de relatie tussen de ruimtes een maximale visuele interactie biedt.

Este interior debía reunir un espacio de trabajo y un espacio para la vivienda. La falta de complejos de la propietaria supuso una gran ventaja para el arquitecto, que pudo plantear un proyecto desinhibido, donde la relación entre las estancias facilitara la máxima interacción visual.

Questo interno doveva riunire uno spazio di lavoro e uno spazio per l'abitazione. L'assenza di complessi da parte della proprietaria ha rappresentato un grande vantaggio per l'architetto, che ha potuto impostare un progetto disinibito, dove il rapporto tra le stanze facilitasse la massima interazione visuale.

Este interior tinha de conciliar um espaço de trabalho e um espaço para habitação. O facto de a proprietária não ter ideias preconcebidas facilitou a tarefa ao arquiteto, que pôde desenvolver um projeto desinibido, em que a relação entre as várias divisões facilita ao máximo a interação visual.

Denna interiör behövde sammanfoga en arbetsyta med ett vardagsrum. Att ägaren inte var rädd för något var till fördel för arkitekten, som obehindrat kunde genomföra ett projekt där förhållandet mellan rummen ger maximal visuell interaktion.

The juxtaposition of original features with newly constructed ones is becoming increasingly common in what is known as "new minimalism".

La coexistence d'éléments originaux avec des éléments nouveaux est à chaque fois plus marquée dans ce que l'on appelle le « nouveau minimalisme ».

Das Zusammenspiel originaler Elemente mit anderen aus neuer Konstruktion sind immer mehr im sogenannten „Neuen Minimalismus" zu beobachten.

Originele en nieuwe elementen met elkaar combineren, komt steeds meer voor bij het zogenaamde nieuwe minimalisme.

La convivencia de elementos originales con otros de nueva construcción está cada vez más presente en el denominado «nuevo minimalismo».

La convivenza di elementi originali con altri di nuova costruzione è sempre più presente in quello che è chiamato il «nuovo minimalismo».

A convivência de elementos originais com outros de construção nova está cada vez mais presente no chamado «novo minimalismo».

Blandningen av ursprungliga detaljer med nybyggda blir allt vanligare i den så kallade "nyminimalismen".

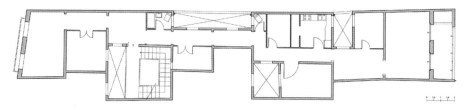

Floor plan before the refurbishment

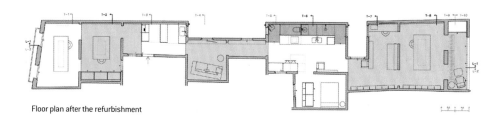

Floor plan after the refurbishment

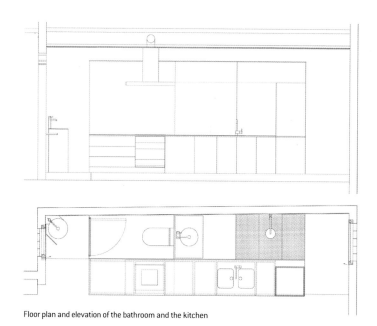

Floor plan and elevation of the bathroom and the kitchen

Semi-transparent glass and the use of white produce diffuse lighting. This helps to prevent a claustrophobic atmosphere in a narrow space.

La transparence partielle du verre et la couleur blanche apportent un éclairage diffus qui élimine l'impression claustrophobe de se trouver dans un espace restreint.

Die Halbtransparenz von Glas und die weiße Farbe schaffen ein diffuses Licht, das das Gefühl von Klaustrophobie in einem schmalen Raum verhindert.

Met semitransparant glas en wittinten behaal je een diffuus licht. Daardoor wordt een smalle ruimte minder claustrofobisch.

La semitransparencia del cristal y el color blanco consiguen una iluminación difusa que evita la sensación claustrofóbica en un espacio estrecho.

La semitrasparenza del vetro e il colore bianco garantiscono un'illuminazione diffusa che evita la sensazione claustrofobica in uno spazio stretto.

A semitransparência do vidro e a cor branca conseguem uma iluminação difusa, que evita a sensação de claustrofobia num espaço apertado.

Halvgenomskinligt glas och vit färg ger en diffus belysning som jagar bort den klaustrofobiska känslan i ett trångt rum.

TOMIGAYA APARTMENTS

SATOSHI OKADA // Tokyo, Japan
© Nácasa & Partners

This building stands in a residential area with heavy traffic. The architect's solution was to use a minimalist design to reduce the visual impact of the surroundings. Several volumes of differing heights and materials were combined; the use of Corten steel in one of the volumes softened the overwhelming effect of the block.

Cet édifice s'élève dans une zone résidentielle où il y a beaucoup de passage. La solution de l'architecte a notamment consisté à limiter l'impact visuel grâce à un design minimaliste. Plusieurs volumes de différentes hauteurs et de matériaux variés ont été combinés, auxquels s'ajoute un volume en acier Corten conçu pour adoucir l'effet étourdissant de l'ensemble.

Dieses Gebäude wurde in einer Wohngegend mit viel Verkehr gebaut. Die Lösung des Architekten lag in der Reduktion des visuellen Eindrucks durch ein minimalistisches Design. Es wurden verschiedene Inhalte in verschiedenen Höhen und Materialien sowie das Design eines Volumens aus Cortenstahl kombiniert, das den überwältigenden Effekt des Blocks mildert.

Het gebouw staat in een woonwijk met veel verkeer. Om de visuele impact te verminderen, tekende de architect een minimalistisch ontwerp. Blokken van verschillende hoogte en opgetrokken uit verschillende materialen wisselen elkaar af en een ontwerp van Cortenstaal dempt het verkeersgeluid van de drukke omgeving.

Este edificio se alza en una zona residencial con mucho tráfico. La solución del arquitecto pasó por reducir el impacto visual mediante un diseño minimalista. Se combinaron varios volúmenes de diferentes alturas y materiales, y el diseño de un volumen de acero cortén, que amortigua el efecto abrumador del bloque.

Questo edificio si erge in una zona residenziale con molto traffico. La soluzione dell'architetto è stata quella di ridurre l'impatto visivo attraverso un progetto minimalista. Sono stati combinati vari volumi di diverse altezze e materiali, e il progetto di un volume di acciaio Corten, che smorza l'effetto pesante del blocco.

Este edifício encontra-se numa zona residencial com muito trânsito. A solução do arquiteto passou por reduzir o impacto visual recorrendo a um *design* minimalista. Foram combinados volumes de diversas alturas e materiais com o *design* de um volume em aço corten, que atenua o efeito esmagador do bloco.

Denna byggnad ligger i ett bostadsområde med tung trafik. Arkitektens lösning blev att minska den visuella påverkan genom en minimalistisk design. Man kombinerade flera block av olika höjd och material, och ett block av Cortenstål, vilket dämpar bullret från omgivningen.

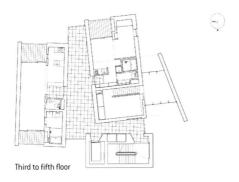

Third to fifth floor

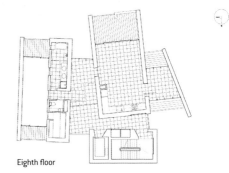

Eighth floor

First floor

Sixth floor

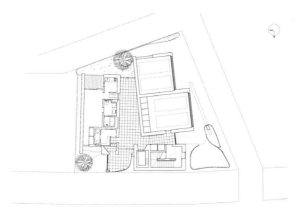

Ground floor

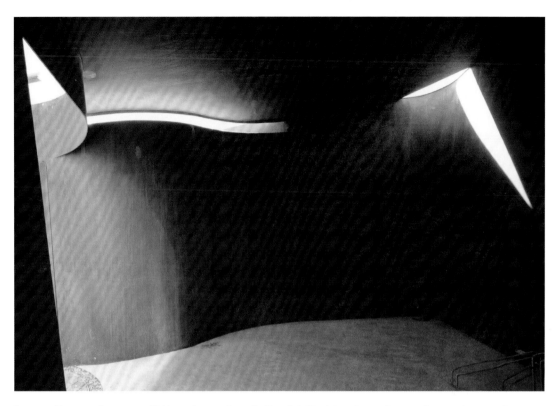

Corten steel is commonly used in homes with minimalist construction to create simple clean forms.

L'utilisation de l'acier Corten dans les espaces de construction minimaliste est courante car il est porteur de formes simples et épurées.

Die Verwendung von Corten-Stahl in minimalistischen Wohnungen ist üblich, da sieeinfache und reine Formen schafft.

Cortenstaal wordt veel gebruikt in minimalistische woningen omdat het zich goed leent voor eenvoudige en strakke vormen.

Es habitual el uso de acero Corten en las viviendas de construcción minimalista ya que permite formas simples y limpias.

È tipico l'uso di acciaio Corten nelle case di costruzione minimalista dato che consente forme semplici e pulite.

Em casas de construção minimalista é habitual o uso do aço corten, que permite formas simples e despojadas.

Det är vanligt att använda Cortenstål när man bygger minimalistiska bostäder eftersom det tillåter minimalistiskt enkla och rena former.

In large buildings constructed with cold materials, it is a good idea to create spaces on a human scale and to take great care with lighting.

Pour les édifices de grandes dimensions, construits avec des matériaux froids, il convient de créer des espaces à échelle humaine et d'apporter un soin particulier à l'éclairage.

In Gebäuden von großer Dimension, die mit kalten Farben gebaut wurden, werden oft Räume nach menschlichem Maß und mit gut durchdachter Beleuchtung geschaffen.

In grote gebouwen opgetrokken uit koude materialen, is het van belang om kleinere ruimtes op menselijke maat in te passen en te zorgen voor een goede verlichting.

En los edificios de grandes dimensiones construidos con materiales fríos, es conveniente crear espacios a escala humana y cuidar bien la iluminación.

Negli edifici di grandi dimensioni costruiti con materiali freddi, conviene creare spazi a misura d'uomo e curare bene l'illuminazione.

Nos edifícios de grandes dimensões construídos com materiais frios, é conveniente criar espaços à escala humana e prestar grande atenção à iluminação.

I byggnader med stora dimensioner uppförda i kalla material rekommenderas det att man skapar utrymmen i mänsklig skala och är noga med belysningen.